UPON ARRIVAL

INCEPTION

John T. Eber Sr.
MANAGING EDITOR

A publication of

Eber & Wein Publishing
Pennsylvania

Library of Congress
Cataloging in Publication Data

ISBN 978-1-60880-627-0

Proudly manufactured in the United States of America by

Eber & Wein Publishing
Pennsylvania

A Note from the Editor . . .

> Mine were my faults, and mine be their reward.
> My whole life was a contest, since the day
> That gave me being, gave me that which marr'd
> The gift—a fate, or will, that walk'd astray;
> And I at times have found the struggle hard,
> And thought of shaking off my bonds of clay:
> But now I fain would for a time survive,
> If but to see what next can well arrive.
>
> —George Gordon Lord Byron
> *from* "Epistle to Augusta" (1830)

Poets and readers, we bid you a warm welcome upon arrival here between these covers where we may speak words most dear. In our next beloved series, poetry gives voice to authors through the universal language of emotions—pains, joys, sorrows, and celebrations—in a safe place to share thoughts, announce successes, and grieve losses with kindred spirits. We use verse to announce the important things, to tell our stories, to witness for the record events that matter most: tragedy, loss, and frustration but also love, admiration, and the peace of nature. Here, no topic is off-limits or ignored. Poetry permits us to tell our stories, heal from our pain, and celebrate our successes. The task does not always come easy, but the reward is release, relief, and accomplishment.

Sometimes in our lives we are stirred by feelings so deep, so gut-wrenching—good or bad—that we must tap ourselves with pen and let the excess overflow onto paper. You have turned the page onto neutral ground for those important expressions, where acceptance can be found among a devoted and passionate community of poetry-enthusiasts. We are from all walks of life, and we come together here to share with mutual respect our creations, from beginners to seasoned veterans. We all struggle to make the right decisions for our loved ones and communities while pursuing the pinnacles of self-actualization and personal fulfillment; let's follow

Lord Byron's lead and look forward to new and unexpected arrivals, of life's challenges and consequent rewards, rather than perseverate on obstacles and negativity.

Some poets exercise careful structure in their work while others employ more organic compositions. Rhyming or not, poems capture language as a living entity and give simple printed words vivacious energy, creating a hallowed covenant between writer and reader—as one cannot exist without the other. Be open to serendipity's pen. "The power which resides in him is new in nature," said Ralph Waldo Emerson, "and none but he knows what that is which he can do, nor does he know until he has tried." You can't always predict the effect words will have on you, but be persistent and you will arrive on the other side with compassion, love, and life vicarious.

We are continually humbled by the honesty, bravery, and talent of our contributors. Poets great and small all contribute to the noble task of weaving history with humanity, preserved in print, to inspire and embolden the future. We thank you, writers and readers alike, and extend our deepest appreciation to all for keeping poetry alive, opening your hearts, and confiding your experiences—from which we may all learn and grow.

Desiree Halkyer
Editor

Possibly

Palsied hands knit the threads
of my life's mission on a shattered shuttle,
a doomed loom whose stitches pick out
scenes of madness and sanity in league.
Dream fugues draw down
their painted lampshades
and the dance of Dusk's denizens intercedes—
moths play ecstatically with flames,
bats beam the heavens for prey
and the 'possum clans stay hidden
and hunkered down until
not. A moon-round door opens in the side
of the windy, harsh-tongued night.
Coyotes loop their howls around the far
constellations while owls
pronounce a downy dharma one by one
from tree to swaying tree—call… response.
Sometimes you'll feel the family of it all:
The exquisite symmetry of everything living,
the chaos resolved into an organic order as
totem tribes pass their secret ways of learning the world
from flock to hatchling, pack to cub
down litter upon litter of fresh-eyed fox kits
striding effortlessly along behind their Brushtailed Mother
through the deep, bowled, generous valleys of paradise.

Kyle Matthews
Sebastopol, CA

A Privileged Desire

Rest my weary mind
Enslaved in subdued arrangements
Whilst the flames within me drown.
Who am I if not the one to burn
Through desires with the drive of feet
That trample on my soul?
Hailstones melt amongst my heavy heart.
In flight my wings soar greater
Than the corporate beast
That clips and clamps them down,
A featherless dove was once a flourished eagle.
Return to me the fire and the blood,
The creation of a body and soul
That lives and wakes in dreams.
A lion heart with rabbit eyes
I take back wthat which is truly mine— I can.

Melissa Lee Ribaudo
Beckenham, Kent

Broody on the Beach

She watches, brooding, the child with the sandy hair.
Wishing, that one day, she could bring her child there.
He plays in the sand, in his little blue shorts,
As greed becomes her, consuming her thoughts.
For she is the one, out of all of her friends,
That shall never be content, never find an end,
To her search for happiness. So she sits, lonely and bored
As she watches envious, noticed, yet ignored.
She preys on others now, a set of three,
Watching them intently, praying that she
Could hold them close, stroke their curls,
Either would be a blessing: boys or girls.
Amongst the pebbles and the algae so green,
A bead of sweat shines on her forehead, glistens, gleams,
As does her burning jealousy, her fiery compassion,
She parades her bitterness it's part of her fashion.
Her tight pulled-back bun, the pristine clothes,
But this is a lifestyle that she has not chose.
For infertility has cursed her so,
And forced her down to the depths below.
She watches, brooding, the child with the sandy hair,
Wishing, that one day she could bring her child there.
But she cannot and will never give her children an ice cream each,
So she takes one last breath, broody on the beach.

Jake Ben Wheatley
Eastbourne, SUSS

Grandpa's Pocket Watch

You won't find Grandpa's pocket watch in a pocket of my jeans
Yet it's always in the pocket of my dress clothes by routine
These days it doesn't work in the ways of a clock
For its stem won't wind, and its tick won't tock
On 12:13, its hands are stuck
Doesn't matter to me, it's pocketed for luck
Engraved in gold, a special date to see
Birth year of a daughter, and a mother named Marie

Ron Rutler
Gardner, KS

In My Private Ocean

I'm swimming in my eyes, in my private ocean
It's hard to see, the shapes, they have no faces, no form or soul
Just dark untouchable memories
The sting of my face, my throat hurts as I sink deeper from the light.
I'm swimming in my eyes—toward nothing; silent, empty
like the dim cold morning after a dying
In my private ocean, I'm swimming in my eyes, alone
You are gone.

Tom Anderson
Hillside, IL

Wicked Game

You played such a wicked game,
it caused me so much shame.
I gave all my trust to you,
I gave my love away,too.

You shattered my heart.
And my world fell apart.
Now I must suffer,
while you're happy with her.

This is so unfair,
to make me think you care.
I still hear your laughter,
so much for happily ever after.

Kiara Tassone
Pawtucket, RI

I am a thirteen-year-old girl who's fought through a lot—mostly family issues. My mom was really sick for a long time. I remember she almost died several times before her life-changing surgery. I suffered from depression for awhile because of this. That's what got me into poetry. I realized the effect words can have on a person, and my life experiences inspire my writing.

The Motherless Child

Children please listen to what I have to say,
Before six feet under one day I will lay.
My mother died when I was eight years old,
The big word LIFE I never heard told.
I was taught and raised in a foster home,
And the one thing was there that I needed and that was love.
I just thank God I never had to use hard drugs or sell my body to
survive.
And thank Him for letting me now be alive.
When you don't have a mother it's a dog-eat-dog world.
People will try to use you and make your head swell.
The key to surviving is being very strong,
Not seeing how many people you can do wrong.
If you all live to be five, twenty five, or thirty five,
Remember future doctors, lawyers
or whatever to be, only the strong survive.

Beverly Perry
Chicago, IL

The Key to My Heart

Someone holds the key to my heart
Unlikely you think and yet true.
A heart's only opened by someone it loves
And, darling, that someone is you.

Just stop for a while and ponder
What a gift it could actually be,
To receive such a thing like somebody's love
By unlocking their heart with a key.

And if you pay real close attention
While unlocking my heart you may find
You not only opened the door to my heart
But also the door to my mind.

It's not to be taken for granted
Or tossed aside on a shelf,
For someone may pick up the key that was lost
While you're looking for it for yourself.

Francine Ross
Cape Coral, FL

The Mamogram

I went to the doctor the other day.
He told me,"You're in the age group;
you need a mamogram right away."
So I headed to the clinic apprehensive as can be.
Now let me tell you what happened to me.
The nurse put my breasts between a clear, plastic vice.
She squeezed and squished them both—
both ways in that device.
As I stood there with tears of pain in my eyes
and helpless as can be, a miserable thought came to me.
What if a fire broke out—would she leave me
in this horrible state? What then would be my fate?
Just then the nurse released them from that plastic plate.
I looked—they were flat, red, and throbbing in pain endlessly.
Oh, how I wished they were not attached to me!
Ah, but only temporarily.
Next the nurse said, as if she couldn't wait,
"I'll see you next year—same place, same date!"
I just nodded my head as I walked out the door.
With a heart full of hate for that breast-smashing
machine forevermore!

Myrna Kinzler
Brownwood, TX

Broken Under Fire

The shadows arch their livid brows at me,
creeping along so sneakily
The angry cuts upon my arm
are staring at me in alarm.
The stripes, they swayed and swooned in time
to lulling voice
and snakish rhyme
The windows pull us out of dimension,
and endless nothing, in suspension
And shouts! And shouts
come from the void
I cover my ears, but can't avoid
They're chasing me, they're in my head
There's nothing left
but what they've said

Leilani Ray
Ladson, SC

*I wrote this poem at a major turning point in my life when acceptance of letting
go of the past was necessary in order to propel forward in my life.*

Repulsed

One warm Orlando summer night
remember those who died tonight
left this world through devils gate
another senseless act of hate
no one deserves to die this way
don't let these cowards get away
only you can save the day

Nothing anyone can say
is changing what we saw here
give us a chance to conquer fear
how then do we contemplate?
tell those who live with blame and hate
come together
let's see this through
unite! Defeat these killing few
bring together not apart

Make our country strong and smart
all we need is to unite
save your hate your strength your might
stop the rift that's caused by fear
against others who are here
come together let us start
reach down deep within your heart
everything we need to do! Stay united - me with you

Ian Rowdy Rowan
East Hampton, NY

Represent God Almighty

Represent, represent, it's time to represent
Stop the hate!
Stop the rage!
Stop the murder in the street!
Start the healing!
Start the giving!
Start the living!
For each other!
Fathers are mourning!
Mothers are crying!
Our children are dying in the street!
Break the fever!
Break the curse!
Heal the scars!
Mend the heart!
Give your soul back to God.
Look at the picture.
Look at it well—drive-by shootings everywhere
Young people dying and going to jail
Selling babies for a rock, shooting people you don't know why
Popping needles in their veins—selling cocaine!
And that's a shame!
Can't you see the signs of time
Christ is going to crack the sky—it might be tonight
Can't you see it's the devil wanting us to kill each other!
Represent, represent, it's time to represent God
Because you don't want your soul going up in smoke, it's a seal
spells out Hell

Chanda DuBose
Davidson, NC

The DR Now

Years ago I fell in love
   with you
I thought you were my
Prince Charming
Little did I know you
   would hurt me too
And make my life so alarming

Well, I've gotten older
and see what you will do
I've gotten a lot bolder
and can walk away from
   you

I love myself now
and know I deserve better
So all I can say in this
letter is
It's O.K. now

Arthenia Franks
Mobile, AL

Blind

If the Spirit above made us all blind;
Instead of seeing color we would look to the mind
Of those we persecute for the color of their skin
And maybe realize that as the human race we all are akin.

here is good and evil in all who walk the earth.
We all are given choices from the time of our birth.
Someday we will all be judged; you and me.
When no one is looking, what will He see?

As for me, I will see with my heart.
It won't be perfect, but it's a start.
Be it sir or be it dame,
Six feet under we all look the same.

Lee Scribner
Wurtsboro, NY

The Year of the Bird

Part 1
There is so much excitement in Baltimore Ravens
Energy grows, adrenaline is pumping in early fall
Heartbeats quickly, as pulse rates reach high altitudes
Drums are thumping, fans are singing true
We are the Baltimore Ravens
When we come to play defensive football
There are no safe havens
Opposing offensives will not forget the days
When they played football games against the Baltimore Ravens
We have been knocked around a time or two ourselves
But we will raise the claw and remain standing
Let us sing this birdville bop
This is the play call
Welcome to Birdville, the year of the birds
Where the team trains in hard knocks
Let is sing,
A Baltimore bird that forever rocks
We are the Baltimore Ravens and our football
and can forever flocks
playoffs are grandiose here in Baltimore
Crowned two superbowls and growing
Quote the Raven evermore

Jonathan Steele
Sharpsville, PA

To You With Love

To you with love
Your all I have
Heart and soul
Happy and sad

To you with love
You fill my dreams
You are my prince
Your here with me

You fit my hand
Just like a glove
And so I write this
To you with love

Leesa Collett
Rock Island, IL

Colorado Weather

One day there's sun
Next day there's none
Sometimes it drizzles
Next day it fizzles
Then there is snow
and surely I'll know
It will either be deep
or be gone as I sleep
No one can say
What the weather will be
The only real answer
Is wait and you'll see.

Joan C. Damp
Westminster, CO

Let Us Go

Let us go now, you and I, into the sweeping field
Where sweetly scents permeate the air
And high the flower yield

Let us go now, you and I, into the whispering wood
Tall trees reaching down to grab
If only that they could

Let us go now, you and I, into the biting cold
Where frozen tendrils grasp my heart
Sure in their icy hold

Let us go now, you and I, into that dark abyss
Where fire consumes all things
And all things are amiss

You must go now, you, not I, back into the light
For deepest sleep has taken me
This dark and lonely night

Adam Taylor
McKenzie, TN

For a Marine

For a marine, his head is full of intelligence and confidence, but his heart can mislead a woman's feelings for him and has a way to develop a woman's low self-esteem.

For a marine, he's good at saying sorry when he knows he can't promise to be honest about it.

For a marine, I could see that even though the love I have for him will remain in my heart, he cannot be the man I want to call my soulmate, my true love, my future husband, or my everything.

This marine was known to be my best friend, my deepest love, the one guy I don't want to stop loving.

In the future, he might be out of my life forever, but as for now, my heart still beats for him.

Tamera Edley
Farmville, VA

George Montag

After years the cancer took control
He was a rose between two ugly thorns
Father of seven, always on patrol
Refusing the treatment, ready to morn

Forgetting to eat or drink, that's not good!
Repeating over and over and over again
Forgetting more and more, but there he stood
Hurting so much but rarely complained

Eighty-one and hurting worse, day after day
Lasting one more year, then passing in June
Though he was in pain, he felt it necessary to play
After the funeral, Daddy's Hands was a sad tune

Eighty-two and gone, no longer distressed
With his spouse again, and happy at rest

Andrea Jinsky
Wisconsin Rapids, WI

Holding the Beast

Trying to hold the
  beast from coming out
from within. Controlling
  from going out.
Walking softly past
  those that
  want to awaken the beast.
  Changing me into a wild
dog sicken with rabies.
Keeping away from the
full moon of ignorance.
Taking deep breaths to
calm the beast from
  ripping out from within.
But the moon with all
  its hate continues to try
to turn me
  into that beast that
smells the blood
of revenge trying to
  kill the one
  that hunt the one who wants
to hurt the beast.
Holding on to the
  silver cross
  that calms and controlls
  the beast
from within me.

Wilfredo Gomez
Queens, NY

A Bird on a Limb

A bird, on a limb, chirping...
sent me on my way, laughing...
when I had planned to be mad
all day long.

George Giffin
Canton, MI

Untitled

Life buds forth anew
Earth awakens from its sleep
Innocence is born.

Kathleen S. Shirar
Antioch, CA

Eager Heart

I'm learning to love.
Fear delays my young hearts growth.
However, desire wins!

Theodore M. Holman
Tacoma, WA

The Plan

Once upon a midnight when I was at my low.
   I dreamed I was in the woods, and knew not where to go.
If I would take a step or turn myself around
   Whatever choice I would take, I would lose some ground.
I know life is a gamble, and some are bound lose.
   But what has happened in my life is not what I would choose.
Although I may be at a low, the only way is up.
   And I'll take steps to get on top, no ifs, no ands, or buts.
When I do I'll share with you the way that life must be.
   And live our life as man and wife, just you the dog and me.

Regis R. Bell
Allison Park, PA

Broken Heart

Like a ferocious lion trapped in a cage
I am forcedto contain my rage.
I stare out of my window
watching the rain pour down
no amount of make up
can hide my forlorn frown.
I should have seen it coming right from the start
in anger I break the window
like you broke my heart.

Morgan Blundell-Smith
Coventry, WMID

One Moment

I'd love to snatch a moment
Of the happy times of life
And save it near to guide me
Through dark, unpleasant strife.

I'd want to grasp it sometime
When the joy as at its best
And keep this special moment
Set aside from all the rest.

I'd hold it closely near me
And use it as my bail
When trouble comes a' knocking
And my efforts seem to fail.

I'd always keep it with me
So when the world was cold
It could be my firm supporter
And my strong and steady hold.

I'd keep it hidden safely
Like a special little treasure
To bring to sadder moments
Just a little bit of pleasure.

I'd love to make this possible
If only it could be.
It would open up a dream house
And I would own they key.

Jeanne Eanes
Valdosta, GA

My Purple Girl

She lives in a purple House
With a purple Dog and a purple Frog
Purple Papaya is her favorite fruit
She drinks her purple wine
She always lives in a purple Haze
With her purple hair in the air
A purple Moon with purple Beans
Are Shining through her purple Stars
And her Purple Eyes Shine On & On
She wears pink paisley paints
With pink purple Polka-dotted ties
She only likes Purple People Eaters
The Sun purple clouds hang over
The Purple Sun in the Purple Rain
In her perfect purple World

Steven Eugene Whittington
Rohnert Park, CA

Snow, Big Deal

Looking outside, well wadda ya know!
Joking aside, hell, gotta be snow...

Tiniest fragments of delicate froth,
finest of figments descend from aloft!

An eerie silence, out here abounds
Air fairly misty—all here surrounds

Branches of trees covered in white
Chances one sees a wonderful sight.

Tall oaks, the black skeletons in pallid skies
Small 'blokes', we lack reflections on paltry lives

Our yearly four seasons, truly 'splendiforous'
For clearly more reasons, not only coniferous

Hope everyone enjoys this season over there
Coping, having fun, employs good reason and care.

Dot Smyth
Bella Vista, AR

Breaking Apart

I fell for you at the start,
But then you broke my heart.
You literally left me in tears,
And left me to face my fears.
You used me just for sex,
But what else should I expect?
For you I broke down my walls,
Answerd all your drunken calls
And after all my care,
I don't know how you dare,
Leave me standing outside your house,
Quietly weeping into my blouse.
And not even feeling dread,
Knowing the thoughts that go on in my head.

Vera Tsupahhin
Naas, Kildare

Colours So Free

Activity creativity activity creativity
The sense of wow the thought descends
Configures through my brain to hands
Pictures images colours trends
Dispelling channelling to easel stands
So others catch the fire the pain
Turn it to themselves to gain
Help insight something new
To say 'oh I have had it too'
The fire the joy the tranquil scene
They've tasted life and come to me
Through brush and stroke on canvass free

Pam Mary Mills
Dorking, SURREY

Forever in Your Mind

If I shall die tomorrow
Would your heart feel any sorrow?
For my mind and body may be gone,
My spirit will forever live on.
You will see I can never be lost forever
In the heart of thee.
Because things that happen will constantly remind you of me.
As I stand at heavens gates I
shall forever wait for you to join me at another date.

Mary Rusher
Newton, IA

The Terror in Nice

Savagery the sight clearly sees yet blear is the state of mind
Beyond such pain, numbness ensues
the shredded spirit is left behind
Shrieking voices hit notes
no musician could rival
To relive the horror such as
is the curse for any survival
Unnatural destruction had passed your path
where ruins bore the deepest of wound
Be healed in no time! Rid of the loath!
Meet the days ahead to mend
And gloat,
gloat proudly
Anew to your former glory!

Andressa Villa
London, Greater London

Mother Nature

It's sad to say but our Mother is dying,
so of her gifts we must stop relying,
We've massacred her pets and ravaged her garden,
now her discipline is beginning to harden,
She's given fair warning killing millions with ease,
using floods typhoons and disease,
We must act now before nothing is left,
except pain suffering and regret,
We must realise her resources will run out,
even if it's 100 years or thereabout,
We can start now it's not too late,
to stop the carnage we create,
We can replace the trees and stop the wars,
it can be like it was before,
Lush green lands where animals are free,
we need to stop the anger and greed,
If we change one thing at a time,
off her deathbed our Mother may climb.

Steven McBride
Newton Aycliffe, Durham

Poetry

Remember back in kindergarten
when you were taught to read
It opened up a whole new world
that you would surely need
That's exactly how I felt
when I started writing poetry
It used to just be something
to do instead of class
But now it has become my own class
that I work to pass
I used to write for grown ups
but now it is for me
Oh so many different words to try
and make it rhyme
Using unique rhythms every single time
Every night I try to sleep
with words flying through my head
It happens every single time
I try to go to bed
When I wake up I write it all down
with a pencil full of lead
I guess this happens to anyone
who has poetry in their head!

Asher Zumwalt
Davidsonville, MD

The Ghost of 2016

everyone I love ends up in hospital bed
like dolls carefully placed along shelves
lined up, smothered in wires and washing
down the pills they are fed
everyone I love has kissed death by dancing along
a line of traffic or having one too many bottles
what they don't know is the more they fill
themselves with poison,
the more empty they become
everyone I love has given up
and told me that I am not what I used to be
that I am merely a shell with the same heart
just colder than before with a chest that caves
when I can no longermuster up the words that
I am happy to be alive
everyone I love has gone away
and I am left here,
what used to be my suburban kingdom
is now the same four walls
that remind me of everything I used to have
everything I used to be
and the worst part is that I'll never go back

Eli Parker
Port Jefferson Station, NY

Sleepless Nights

A happy life, a happy marriage, a happy family
What could go wrong? The phone is ringing
Someone just died; it's their only child
Hope this doesn't ruin their perfect life
Hope there won't be any sleepless nights
"Time heals all wounds"
"You're in our prayers"
The words of comfort sent their way
but nothing could numb their pain
The wife comes home from a night of drinking and fights
She screams and laughs, screams and laughs
making the whole house rise
For a sleepless night
Husband and wife are arguing
They fought all night so he took a flight
Her perfect marriage now blown up in the wind like a kite
I don't think she's getting any sleep tonight
Her lover's gone, don't want her no more
Is it really her fault? Does she have to mourn?
Yet she cries and cries, cries and cries
For another sleepless night
Sleepless night, sleepless night
The perfect life is now over
Too many bad things happened
On a sleepless night

Favour Igiebor
Bronx, NY

Intertwined

I am your calm in the storm as you are mine
Whenever I feel empty and dull
You fill me up and make me shine
When we met it was like the stars had aligned
I was yours and you were mine
Our lives had been forever intertwined
In one moment, of extreme bliss
With the start of just one kiss
I could never dismiss
The love I feel for you
In my heart I know that's it true
Over the years my love has grown
To a feeling that I have never known
I hope that over the years that I have shown
How much you mean to me and that you are never alone
Together I will stand with you through the storms
And just know my love will always be here to keep you warm
Through it all there is no one I would rather be with
Happily ever after's are just a myth
True love takes work every day
To keep one another's days from being gray
But bright full of promise, full of hope,
Full of laughs, full of smiles,
Just as it was the day we walked down the aisle
I am yours and you are mine
Our lives are forever intertwined

Quiana Zellner
Lexington Park, MD

Stitches

Torn apart by wrath
One are now two
Separates warmth
Bloods cold blue
Battered long before
This but he knew
When why I did adore
He with whom I grew
Greatly did I give
For granted it was took
Admission to be hid
In charismatic of a look
Cherished love behold
The place I carry he
Alive within my soul
Toxic as can be
Tongue lashes without care
Removing every stitch
Emotionally bare
Drained by every inch
True love was once the claim
If ever that were true
Sewing broken pieces
Was all he had to do

Angela Story
Bryson City, NC

Passing Time

Its seems like just yesterday I was on the school playground,
Being a little girl, enjoying life.
Now it is almost time for me to go off and leave this town
And to think that soon then I will be somebody's wife.
It is crazy how day after day, I see the moments pass by.
Sometimes I wonder how I may,
Capture and try to enjoy all the seconds that fly.
I know that right now is all that there is,
But sometimes I forget to live in the moment.
I am scared that I will fail to grasp it like a pop quiz.
I just want to live life, caught up in enjoyment.

Ashley Mendoza
Miramar, FL

Lack of Passion

It's like you want someone to waste time with
Not someone to grow with, it's not all bad
We talk, we laugh
But there's a lack of passion, no foundation
Not building to last is building to break
I want the minutes, days, and hours with you
But only if you want that too

Taylor Hamilton
Willingboro, NJ

Don't Make No Mistakes

What are you doing making another mistake?
How can you say it's love?
When we don't understand
When they try to help you you want to put them down.
Next thing you know you're now the one looking like the clown.
You want to think and hope that they are the one.
But when your name come to their mind they think
you're just for fun.
Like they always say nothing ever comes for free.
So we have to work hard for everything we want work hard indeed.
Forget about all these people because you really don't need them.
Only person you need is Jesus and make sure you keep him.
Put your trust in him because he his going to always be there.
You can fall in love with him don't ever be scared.
He won't take advantage of you and he'll never leave your side.
He is always there to love you and provide.
Never forget this saying, "God is love."
So when you're in need just look up above and know that he is there.
Looking down and will always be with you even until the end.

Leshell Janiece Johnson
Houston, TX

Rough Edges

Rough stabbing edges the endless nights
of painful thoughts
demons trying to hold you down
you keep on looking looking around
keeping all your cries to yourself
the pain is getting longer
the feeling's lasting longer
you think and you wonder
about your life is it real is it right
to sit and think about your life
wondering where to go from here
then your eyes begin to tear
thinking if you were only here
to save me from this painful fear

Mark Donald Jones
Rancho Cordova, CA

How to Raise a Child

To fit in with society
To conform to propriety
To respect others in a crowd
No matter if they're loud
Mom overprotective?
Or her words ineffective?
It is very tough, as we reflect
To rear a child...correct.

Rachel Virginia Levanen
Yacolt, WA

Six Minutes

Six minutes is all you get
Is it over yet?
Barrel to your head
Dare to do it and you're dead
Some will beg, some will plead
They're the ones that made you bleed
Tears rolling down your face
You're the one that they replaced
Six minutes is what you get
Is it over?
Yes

Essie Murphy
Bailey, CO

The Staircase

The staircase next to the lunchroom
Full of passing people's apathy.
Alone, she keeps her tray full
Staring for twenty seven minutes
At the white cinder-block walls
And the railing that separates her from death.
She contemplates eating and looks down.
Her thighs suppress her thoughts
And her mind begins to wander.
It wanders to a world where she isn't alone.
A world where she's happy.
The bell rings.
Her full tray stays with her thoughts
And the apathy of passers-by
In the staircase next to the lunchroom.

Ben Underwood
Holliston, MA

Catastrophe Awakens

Morality plummets
Chaos uprises with rock and fire
Eruption of anarchy

Did not listen
Past errors duplicate
Violence, sickness, deaf became allies
under one sole
King Misery, hail King Misery
Normality is overthrown, cast to the unknown
A contrast sight, contrast context, contrast complex descriptions
The unraveling ensues, depict for oneself
Share my senses
Fear and despair for the living

Fate?
Destiny was always forsaken
Now earth shakes from the bottomless and unseen
But above
Whispers from blackened smoke a golden voice
Divinity punctures the clouds
A raging gape of light descends
for a split second
Hope

Elijah Mosley
Philadelphia, PA

Swan's Death

Moring ripens sunshine
a moor cottage
sails sing no more
thistle summer comes to an end
in my heart never mends

Brad Rothwell Tucker
N. Eastham, MA

Who Am I?

Indulge the sweet juicy nectar string part sector
dulcet wee drip
caress your lip
A distinct fragrance very rare
hard to compare
scopa choring
pollen storing
Multicolored succulent vine
a teasing dine
fetching chuckles
honeysuckles

Donna Roberts
Homosassa, FL

His Eyes

Sometime I don't know why,
I miss you and start to cry.
I've lost some but it's not the same,
I was close to you, I knew your pain.
I feel so strange; it's not what I expected.
We weren't family but we were connected.
I held your hand and prayed to God,
I looked at you and saw you nod.
I saw something in your eyes,
I don't know why it makes me cry.
I have no clue what it meant,
I only hope you were heaven sent.
I want to sleep the whole night though,
It might have bearing on my mood.
I cannot say where or why,
I go to sleep and see your eyes.

Camille A. Allen-Weimer
Green Bay, WI

Dedicated to Contagious Words

The chips are down, the match is struck,
We leave blissful life in a dusty truck.
Sort of...
More like...
Where am I going and what will I be,
The future holds secrets and it won't betray its deeds.
When I look to my past I see stories and dreams,
But I look to the future, see nothing but seams,
Stitches that bind us together (it seems).
And trees
If I dare to make symbols that fit in a box,
Says the lonely young hipster with not but old words,
I would tie us to the trees,
As their roots give them strength,
And their branches their beauty.
Words
Their irresistible tendency to induce rambling,
To the victim of this audacious psychological gambling.
I believe this was supposed to rhyme,
Though I guess my words just didn't leave the time.
Bare feet slap wet sand,
Those feet and sand go hand in hand.
Skipping in the memories of sunny shore,
You know the ones, the ones that dance inside your head,
The ones that lead you through that mysterious wardrobe door.
You know the ones.

Aidan McLean Howard
Kansas City, KS

You Can Find Me in the Cracks

On the sidewalk of my childhood, you can
Find me in the cracks where the dust of the past
Had settled and the rough edges smoothed over
With the rains. The neglected streets seem unapologetic,
Knowing they have suffered more, given more
And gotten less. In the cracks of a tree trunk,
you'll find that youthful song
Of innocence trapped in a time at a brink of tragedy
You can find me in the stagnant air of a residential building
Smelling of old brick and musky cement
There, time stopped in the cracks of the wall
To meet me again in a different form.
What is a crack but a rapture of space and time?
What are memories, then, but collective raptures of space and time?
Yes, find me in the cracks of abandoned matter
Waiting for my day to come
When the bond of knowing and sensing is forever broken.

Anesa Kratovac
Novi, MI

Confessions of a Moth

I was almost a butterfly.
We are of the same order
but I'd rather prefer the night.
What guides me is the bright celestial light,
to which I had a propensity to waft.
I saw my comrades whirl
Around the light with no less than
Lust for the luster.
I derided them as I meandered closer.
I joined them as we danced and
One by one embraced our fates
With a staccato melody.
The zapper, my decision.
The pavement, my firmament.

Alexander Kearns
New York, NY

The Last Note She Ever Wrote

As she draws her destiny up from her spoon
she didn't know or see her end was comin' soon
her gut told her no you are too
young and pretty to go, you have so much more life to live
oh your family I'm sure they are willing to forgive
but she ignored her best guts thought
She said **** it I'm do all the dope I just bought
she didn't even see the end coming
she was walking straight to it no she was running
but she ties off her arm it takes her so long
she really meant her family no harm
her gut and mind was almost that strong
but up shot that red stream
but really for her it was her destiny
she pushed in so slow
as if she never wanted to go
but before she removed her murder weapon
as if it was any more a threatening
her eyes close ever so slow
as if she never wanted to go her friends
ran out the door as if they never seen her before
her body lay back nice and slow as if she never
wanted to go her face began to turn purple and blue
she looked as if she was sick with the flu
but really this was life leaving her face
all because she didn't want to share her dope
with anyone in this place!

Natasha Rose Jude
Columbus, OH

Are You Okay?

Scream,
And maybe someone will hear you,
But I doubt it,
No one ever heard me,
But how could they,
Over the police sirens and car horns,
And the persistent knocking at the front door.

I didn't leave my room that night,
I didn't leave my room the next day,
I didn't watch as they cuffed him and drove away,
I didn't watch anything,
I didn't hear anything,
I didn't taste anything.

New voices visited every day,
Every single damn day,
"Are you ok,"they say,
                No,
"Yes," I say,
                How could I be ok?,
"Why wouldn't I be,"I say,
"You wanna talk about it?"They ask,
"There is nothing to talk about, I'm fine."
                How could I possibly be fine?
                I'm not fine.

Tara Topden Pemba
Meriden, NH

Emotional Destruction

I can't believe it
        When I saw what I saw
    I couldn't think
    Did you mean to hurt me?
     Can you feel my pain?
             Just think
What if I did it to you,
    Would you hate me?

But then I say to myself,
        Baby don't cry
    Dry your eyes
    Keep your head up
      Because if you fall
                You always have to get up!
Then I say to you
        Do you feel guilty or are you just like the rest of them?
     My first words were what happened?
    It was the consequences of someone's actions
      I reacted in a wrong manner
                But what was I supposed to do?
Look what you've done me
    You've made me so miserable
                Now I feel like I'm invisible...

Andrea Rivera
Brick, NJ

The World

The light fades,
Everyone and everything drifts off to sleep.
Except the carrier.
The one who maintains all the weight, without a noise.
Dead silence in the streets.
Then, a sigh.
Not of relief,
Not of sadness.
Just a sigh.
Exhaustion.
Fear.
Corruptness.
Depression.
Mostly, a fake smile.
A fake cover.
Whatever you call the grass acting green, but being gray.
This sigh came from none other than the Earth.
Being trashed, and taken advantage of its talent.
The day it falls is feared by all.
Except one.

Natalie Grace Kelley
Tampa, FL

Thoughts from a Desk of a Slave

beneath the roof you kept me in,
the roof i was raised in,
the shelter i had for the rainy days
and to escape from the hot sun,
but did i ask for anything else?
you tell me you are gonna take away, everything i have,
but only if you know the roof you gave me is all i have.
take away everything and all i have is you and the hope you give.
why don't you just kill me and let me rest in peace...
you don't see the pain you give me, so then i doubt you are blind
then you can't hear the painful words you say,
and deny that you ever said it.
that makes me think that you are all deaf, mute and blind...
you thought you had to go through pain when you were little,
but what about the pain you're giving
to the mother of the unborn child...
not having what you want for you is pain,
then look at the people who starve for just a peaceful day...

Namira Tahsin Nabi
Houston, TX

Slideshow

Watching the memories come and go like a slideshow.
Seeing viewing all the good and the bad from all the times
I went mad or was sad or even the infamous amount of laughing
to the point of crying.
It surprises me how much I remember.
It makes me miss those times, especially the moments shared with
friends and family and at times I wish things can go back to
those simpler days of before double digit years.
Then again I appreciate all the people
I've met and all the things I've learned.
Looking through the memories I can see how I have
grown and matured, the people that've come and gone,
the experiences that I've had and shared.
It kind of makes me feel old due to the
fact that it makes me realize that
despite all the hards times
everything happens for a reason,
even if you don't realize it at first.
It's either that or I have an old soul.
Which now that I am looking at it again,
the second makes more sense.
It's nice to look back.
Now that I have; how about you the reader, sit back,
close your eyes, take a deep breath, relax, and review your slideshow.

Breanna Nikita Nichols
Tampa, FL

What Is the Ocean?

The ocean is a wonderland that goes up and down
It's a galaxy waiting to be recognized
It whooshes around every day on the same floor
Almost like calm glass floating up and down

Where does it come from?
Where does it go?
Maybe no one will ever know
Or maybe someone has an idea

It has eyes that watch us all,
The waves crashing to up high to see us
But lowering to touch your hand
Maybe it's just mother nature in disguise.

It has no meaning but the meaning we give it
It splashes loud when there's a storm
But splashes silently when there is not
It's just a world we call, "The Ocean"

Shravya Sathi
Andover, MA

The Flower That's Standing Stron

Through the struggles
Through the setbacks
Through the storms
Through the hurt
Through the pain
Through the illness
Through the discouragement
I am a fighter like the protea
because I have been fighting this battle for a long time.
I am a determined gentle giant, like the geranium.
I have the strength, honor, and conviction like the gladious.
Singing through the happy times
Smiling from the memories
Surviving the difficult times
Living in the moment
because I am the
flower that stood strong.

Fredericka Paulette Scott
Greenwood, SC

Incomplete Disarray

I miss the days when our tales were one,
written in a book about us both.
When our stories were intertwined,
but now they have simply unraveled.
So now, with binding torn and remaining pages in disarray,
I am left with one imperfect story.
How could you go, taking everyone's favorite character
along with you?
Without you there is no protagonist,
merely supporting characters sauntering about aimlessly.
How could you leave, taking the prime part of the storyline
with you?
For now that you are gone there is no plot, just a nugatory
and barren setting.
Much better were the days when our tales were one.
So come back, darling, that we may rescript our story
To the way it was meant to be written—
In a novel about the both of us.

Pagan Regnier
Tulsa, OK

Life

Life is a scary place to be,
we're constantly told and programed by society,
but I just wanna be me.
A person who is far from perfect in every different way,
struggling to find my place each and every day.
Life wants us to believe that beautiful is skinny, rich, and hot.
All of these are something I am not.
You see beautiful is excepting and loving who you are,
not by the size of your bank account and the look of your car.
Life is a place where we learn who we are and take God's big test.
Not trying to be rich and famous to figure out who is the best.
Life is where we except and appreciate all that God has done.
He has forgiven our evil ways and gave up His one and only Son.
So when you kneel to pray to God up above,
thank Him for trading His Son for our sins,
and ask Him to fill you with love.
In Heaven we all will be equal and rich at the end of the day.
So don't judge and be yourself is all I need to say.

Justin Dale Perry
Airway Heights, WA

Paint Me a Picture

Paint me a picture filled with passion,
bring me back to a place where I still have personal space;
somewhere, between crazy and cryptic.
I want to break through the disguise
so I can run from your eyes.
Memories break free and try to drown me in my tears.
My thoughts are actually moving at a much slower pace.
Paint me a picture of the pain in my eyes,
see if you can capture my feelings inside.
Slow back down and silently, leave the emotion,
quit trying so hard to put out the fire.
Paint me a picture of the day before I lost my mind
See if it's possible to travel back in time.
I'd love to see my face just before they took me away,
a pretty picture to remind myself I don't want to stay.
Pretty pictures need to be framed, they need to be on display.
Paint me a picture of the day I was shackled and taken away.
Paint me a picture of the day I lay there alone,
eyes wide and dazed.
Paint me a picture of the day before I was sick,
I can't recall a memory of it.
Paint that pretty picture and leave it at my door.
Paint it, frame it, just so I'll believe it.

Janey Elizabeth Stevens
Liberty, MS

Essence of Soul

A wind shifts in the ocean of time
A melody is constructed; created to rhyme
It pours out like water and passion aflame
It speaks its existence and resounds its name
It cannot be detered from its purpose
It cannot be held in esteem as worthless
Its power is of its own great command
Its echo is shouted forth as of its own demand
It is not in the waters of the river
It dwells not in the salt of the sea
It cannot be revealed in the heart of a deciever
It isn't found in the shadows that cannot see
It isn't found in the seat of hell, circles seven
The foul voices speak it not, to their own shame
It is found in the heights of the heaven
The stars burn in their zeal to explain
Where its steps are found underneath the burning sun
creatures gather round and whisper what it has done
The hearts of men can only hope to abide in its presence
It erases the sin and consumes all darkness and its essence
It is love, of which all that was has ever sung
It is hope, of which was in all things ever done
It is peace, in which all source of joy abides
It is mercy, in which all zeal and doubt hides

Samuel Stark
Dothan, AL

The Truth?

He was only thirteen when he got jumped
over a phone, but he didn't let up.
Now he's eighteen, living his life the same as always,
Drug deals and smoking, doing anything to get paid.
He *was* someone I *knew*, but now I'm not so sure.
All he knew was hardships, all he knew was being poor.
Now he's like a lord, everyone wanting something from him.
He has a little brother who might end up like him.
I just hope he gets straight and doesn't end up dead in the pen.
He *was* someone I *knew*, but now I'm not so sure.

Selena Renea Henderson
Nashville, TN

Approach of Planet X

thirty-six long centuries count the journey
your orbital path gargantuan mass
passing dangerously near
upsets nature's law poles invert, crust slips
our known world forever lost
on evolving Earth Nibiru, are you
progress catalyst, beyond
popular belief?

Sarah E. Merryman
Bloomington, IN

I Think I Love You

You were always there,
Even when I didn't want you.
You were the sunshine to my darkness,
I never realized what you were to me.
Now that I have lost every one,
And everything I realized you really are the one.
I wanted to love you,
But I didn't know how.
I think I love you.
You left me,
With good reason.
I had no choice but to move on,
And so I did, not realizing what I was losing.
Giving up on everything I had.
I thought I didn't love you.
You appeared in my class,
Sat right next to me like old times.
I had thought it was old news,
I thought you were old news.
I began to tremble at your voice,
Forgot how to love,
But it all came back.
I love you.

Davan Seth-John Hanley
Hershey, PA

The Tree of Love

I am as a tree of winter
Leafless, barren, desolate
The wind howls unlike my soul
The cold consuming my entirety
The leaves like my hope are no more
Incomparable is the dead winter
Alas the soul thaws as the bark of early spring
Branches of love grow strong
Blooming leaves of love allow sight
For the tree of love recovers the winter's presence
The tree will last for so long
Love's branches will be bare again
Its presence in the cold anew
Hope grows in place of love
For hope rescues even the most blue

Nicholas Steven Saccaro
Woodworth, LA

Untitled

My mother is of the ocean.
She was pulled from its depths and
birthed onto our dry, cracked Earth.
Her roots spread,
wide enough to know the land,
to know her mate,
her kin,
her blood,
Earth blood
but wet as the ocean. Here she taught us,
like Mercury,
to be fluid and frenzied, roiling like the sea.
"Stay steadfast but know uncertainty."
When we're ready she'll let us go and
slip silently home.
Plunging head first back into her skin.
We'll stay wondering, watching the tide roll in.
Sea foam licking our limbs.
Her touch,
Her kin,
Her blood,
My blood,
wet as the ocean.

Thryn Saxon
New York, NY

My Promise Keep

Heaven is broken
God is at war with God
Life is rare
The vast empty heart of God
Is broken
Each half is angry
With the other
Divine tears drain
Into a great salt sea
A wounded God sleeps
By the great salt sea
Let God sleep
God has been God
For a long time
Let God rest
Let God dream a love dream
Of a savior rare I promised God
Warmful and gentle sleep
I will not disturb God
When God awakens
All hearts will be unbroken
And my promise keep

Joel Trejo
Houston, TX

Broken and Alone

She was quiet because
she had been here before,
when things started
to unravel and fall
apart at the seams.
She thought this time
was different,
but that proved untrue.
All the bad memories
of her past came breaking through.
She gave her heart yet again,
but as time went by,
it was broken again.
One little lie and a half truth,
had caused her to doubt even the truth.
She tried to forget,
even though she forgave,
but the trust was
lost and could not be regained.
Now she sits in the
reality of the truth,
with tears on her pillow and
her heart in a grave.

Wendy Sue Stinson
Palestine, AR

Don't Look

Misshapen fate draws emotions
tears into that weak wall
ripping apart my devotions
making feeling visible to all
forcing me vulnerable and raw
my private mind:bare
straight inside me I saw
that you can see I care
the mask has fallen from my eyes
now you see what I really feel
away from all the lies
slammed into all that's real
how scared I am to be alone
all the hidden fears
my life in a different tone
instead of smiles you see my tears
please turn away from my vulnerable soul
close your eyes to this sight
believe that I'm really whole
and think I'll be alright

Amy Scheeler
Savannah, GA

The Most Dangerous Place

The most dangerous place used to be the safest
Nourished, cherished by her from whom we came
Any hidden nightmares her soothing voice chases
Protected from harm we silently sang

But now in the darkness quiet hope turns despair
The moans and the groans just fall on deaf ears
Their innocent blood shed without even a care
Weeping, wailing, no one sees countless tears

No chance at life given, light from their eyes taken
No chance for their wildest dreams to come true
The most dangerous place ought to be the safest
Sacrifice for them as was done for you

Jacob Olson
Rice, MN

I Betrayed the Sea

I never thought I would betray the sea.
Fracture our promise through its very core
The essence of beauty was clear to me
My once fulfilled self, yearns for something more
Music from shells no longer ring as sweet
I've left the soothing mix of salt and air
And abandoned the sand against my feet
Forgot a sky I thought could not compare
The sacred vow between us is broken
I've found another shade to admire
Easier to leave with words unspoken
But I cannot hide my new desire
I betrayed the sea when I saw his eyes
So blue, so green, my God, they mesmerize.

Kelly Cecelia Bright
Morrisville, NC

Black Is Beautiful

Why does the color of my skin disgust you?
Why does the slang in my voice make you feel uncomfortable?
Even my curves and hips are a disgrace.
I'm not as attractive as the Caucasian female you so admire.
Just because my skin is infused with rich melanin
You say I'm not at your level of satisfaction.
"Look at the girl with the afro," she can't sit with us
They would say and giggle to themselves.
The complexities of my complexion will never be understood
by those who just look at me with hatred within.
My skin has been ostracized and made fun of to the point
I had to just stop and think;
I just say to myself, baby girl embrace your beauty.
Your rich, dark skin is stunning.
Your African traits are a wonderful sight to see.
Let your melanin pop and shine; you are beautiful outside and within.
Forget about those who think the pigment of your skin is an issue—
Black is magical, black is beautiful, black is me!

Phyllis Marie King
Tuscaloosa, AL

Blade of Grass

Oh blade of grass
Neither coming nor going
Alone, no fruit to bare
Cut short, no seeds to share
Through wind, snow and rain
You forever remain
Woe to you, oh blade of grass

Aaron Lewis
Erie, PA

Undying Love

Still,

    as the Sakura blossoms fall,
    so my spirit slowly fades.

    when the last petal falls,
    I have nothing left to give.

    Yet, I love you still.

Kiyomi Akiko Masami Angel Saffell
Jasper, AL

A Distant Journey

I think I knew before I understood
The intensity of what I could not see.
I felt her resonant loneliness
And her pain
But those feelings I could not explain.
We smile as we talked about
Insignificant Nothings
And as her eyes shifted
About the room
Her thoughts imbued in the
Fragile discontent of the sadness
I could almost touch
Encapsulates my defenses
Taking my breath away.
Her innate affections shattered
In her inability to convey
What she really wanted to feel.
Instead my love for her crumbled
Into mournful weeping
And the humble words that could
Have been spoken between a
Mother and her daughter
Remain dormant in time.

Sandra Maria Rivera
Bronx, NY

Love

Love lays its open
Arms
On everything with an open
Heart.

To find and cherish
Memories,
To make a childhood one of
Dreams.

Haven Suzanne Shedd
Chicago, IL

The World Beyond

I who see the window pane
tell you who see the light
that grass and mud have stained the world
and demons rule the night

But you who know the world beyond
whisper in your sleep
that I need only sacrifice
the eyes I wish to keep

Leela Manya Langlois
Novato, CA

I Wish to Hear Your Song

Sweet little lark, feathers made of starlight,
visited me carrying sunset on his shoulders.
What is the weight of the clouds you carry,
that plunge between your shoulder blades?
I see Orion whispering secrets, tales
of the cosmos ruffling as you preen.
But you remain silent as the galaxies,
as beautiful as the water-color streaks trailing you.
Do you not sing because the sky is your cage,
captive, in pace with the hull you brace against?

Sweet little lark, feathers made of starlight,
visit me again,
carrying sunset on your shoulders,
and stay with me until your captor fades,
releasing the stars from your wings
and spilling the sunset like tears.

Sing.

Emory Larson
Woodbury, TN

All I Have to Offer

There is not much of me;
I should have put more of me into the act of living,
but the loss would have been too great
to bear.
I am shut tight, bolt and lock;
there are reasons for words like *dying*.
For example,
they were born in the belly of
a woman, at the birth of the world.
I bleed in sympathy,
for I, too, am always losing myself in parts
and giving others away.
Take my hand, my breath,
my teeth, my breast—
all I have to offer, a meager sum of a human life.
I breathe and I breathe and I breathe
and for the air I consume—I grieve.
Through locked jaw I speak
with the ferocity of one acquainted with devils.
I know the truths that were previously masked.
There is nothing so smooth it cannot be scratched,
nothing so innocent it cannot be marred,
nothing so precious it is exempt from death.
Here is all I have to offer—
a body, a life, a poem.

Suzanne A. Picinotti
Charleroi, PA

For Now

No one knows the day which we will go.
No one knows the pain they will undergo.
When you left this Earth to be with Him,
our hearts were broken again and again.
Although grateful for the time we had,
not at all prepared to say goodbye to you, Dad.
Throughout the years your voice was heard.
Father, husband, and brother, always a man of your word.
Your love bestowed through your wisdom and strength.
I can still feel the power of your emotional embrace.
On your birthday we are all gathered here
to celebrate the life you led.
Touching each of us in a different way,
Your presence felt on this notable day.
I can see you here watching this place,
a single tear falling from your face.
Your heart is proud, your soul serene,
comfortable now in your being.
I let go of the answers I cannot find
and trust in knowing you are always on my mind.

Brooke Dials
Folsom, CA

Pretty Feels Like

what spring is supposed to be
pastel patterns lining tablecloths and clear skin and a dress
that opens into a parachute when you twirl around in the grass
no shoes on your feet and your toes between the blades.
the way collarbones are defined in curved lines
boats and bridges crossing the horizon of your shoulders.
earrings that hang like chandeliers with gems twinkling
shifting at angles in reflection with the dimly lit room
into which you glide three feet taller, and they can't look away.
when snow first falls onto a soft ground without melting
a perfect white, crystalline and pure,
and when a boot is first pressed, an identical match is made
evidence that a young girl had her first kiss
from the two pairs of prints facing one another, tips almost touching
one with a deeper indent in the toes.
it's a shadow of a moment, a mirage of true love.
in the morning when the sun rises
the world turns a bright yellow washed over with orange
and you turn your face towards it with eyes closed
butterfly wings lying upon rosy cheeks
and lips placed ever so slightly into a smile.
pressing pause in a moment when eyes are meeting for the first time
a fleeting flash of recognition, continuing into a sureness
only infinite because of the natural beauty being held in between.
the way I felt when he told me the stars reminded him of my eyes.

Ally Ameel
Austin, TX

Death Beckons

Death beckons.
Everywhere I go,
death beckons.
A faint whisper only,
but slowly growing more persistent.
It's present all the time now,
present where it never existed before.
It's there when I wake,
and it's there at dusk.
It's always around,
ever so gently beginning to tug at my soul,
reminding me that the journey
is scheduled to continue.
Death beckons.
Everywhere I go death beckons,
and although intrigued
I am somewhat uneasy.

Tony Parete
Brook Park, OH

Haiku (Mother Sleeps)

cool untroubled breeze
whispers Mother time to sleep—
winter's moon unplugged

Vicky Ann Brocato
Marlin, TX

White Flower

Enemies from absence and the freedom to win,
moving stops to steal,
but blunt to scoff,
new paper to dirty,
and lonliness from a hit;
here is moving knowledge from severity
and new still from the toss—
however, never you give from my window
paradise cursed:
less a shadow but nothing,
stationary,
undone,
and laced unto a single white flower.

George Roso
Newton Falls, OH

The Destruction of Alcohol

Alcohol,
You control my dad like a puppet
Sadly, he can't seem to break from the strings
You cut his wings off and gave him a bottle
Alcohol,
My family has been broken up
You brought death to kiss my grandfather's forehead
That broke me!
Alcohol,
You offered me a hand
I accepted!
I washed away my problems with every sip
Alcohol,
After a while everything was the same
I asked what was beneficial about it?
You said nothing!
Alcohol,
You are just addicting
You are like an anchor that drowns us to the depths of our miseries
Why are you powerful? Its one of many mysteries

Alondra Lizbeth Mares
Chicago, IL

Daydream

I caught the tail of a thought
as it started to slip away
It grew strong and pulled me along
as I watched distraction seep into haze
I was caught up in the wonder
as disbelief started to fade
We spun and trailed off
leaving worry for the grave
But at long last, the time passed
and the minutes evaporated
I let go and it dissipated
leaving nothing more than a memory
which faded into a passing feeling

Shenandoah Sierra
West Covina, CA

A Whisper of Deceit

It started out with a smile
With promises that love would stay awhile
As the nights grew long surrounded by tears
The heart knew that love could not survive many years
Never knowing how words leave the soul grasping for air
Finding out that feelings would not play fair
Love whispered to me that he was never true
And yet somehow it cried don't believe it was you!

Marcella Jane Watkins
Belville, NC

From Mother to Daughter

When I heard your heart beat for the first time.
I knew what a miracle you were.
When I first saw you I knew that god sent me an angel.
You were sent by god himsef.
If there was ever a time you were in pain.
I would do every thing in my power to take it away.
Because you mean every thing in my life that
is good in my life.
I would do anything and every thing to make
your world right and happy in your life.
Because you are my angel sent by god.

Sara Ives
Carrollton, MO

Becoming an Angel

Angels will soon gather together.
to welcome a new face.
Waiting to put on another set of
wings.
in an eternal,happy place.
The spirit will always be below
the clouds.
in hearts it will always stay.
As a creation of beauty begin's
a new journey.
Reuniting with loved ones that
will lead the way.
So when there is sadness.
or even a tear.
Never forget that the spirit
will never disappear."

Patti Hereth
Glenwood, AR

Uncared, Innocent, Discriminated

You took it from me
Stole it
But didn't care
You acted as if you were innocent

You deceive people
Make them believe
You're someone that can be trusted
That can be depended on

Only one
One person knows how you work
Knows what you do
And how you do it

You were once good
But you turned, why?
I don't understand, I can't understand
I don't want to, I'm not willing

I was discriminated
From a world
I thought was mine
Cast away like I was wrong

Jordan Renand Alexandre
Randolph, MA

What's a Poem Worth?

Some say a picture is worth a thousand words.
 Is a poem worth a thousand miles,
 Hiking through the Rocky Mountains of your thoughts?
 Or a thousand sleepless nights
 Debating prose and other nonsensical lyrics?

If a picture has memories that last a lifetime,
 A poem has a message that will last a millennium.

A poem is a baby, newly born,
 With a whole life of contingency ahead of it.
 It is an opportunity
 To share what's on one's mind
 Reaching into the crevice of their heart.

A poem is an adventure.
 A journey in an unknown world.
 It is a breath of fresh air
 To one whose head rose above the waves
 On a cold night.

A poem is a heart and mind,
 Working in harmony to achieve dreams.
 A poem is a person looking for their self-worth.
 A poem that has found its way
 Are thoughts that go from dreams to birth.

Maxx Nichols
Petoskey, MI

Shattered

Aesthetically pleasing sweetheart of mine,
With wind blown hair and skin so fine.
Your chiseled features strike fireworks in my forbidden mind.
Conducting the night with soothing words, how can you be so blind?
Wafting fingers flitter against my back, little drunken men in fame
Arms of magnets engulfing my cold, frail, metal body frame.
Electricity snaps in the room as the sun begins to set.
Our mouths spewing memories like your mothers worn cassette.
Your lips are light roses prickling mine, oh, such endless time.
A skull encrusted with books and maps, forgetting smoke and crime.
Hearts plastered with "I love yous and "please do not cry."
Stomachs exploding night after horrid night with "why do I even try"
A returning pit that consumes my torso presents itself once more,
This cavern of despair has been here before.
You left forgetting to collect your scent from my bed,
An absence of masculine warmth will soon spread.
As a god you assure all hope that these feelings will soon subside,
"Drink some water, it'll all be fine."

Devra Catarena Athanasiadis
Petoskey, MI

The Fall of Love

Love flows
swiftly,
rapidly
along the crevice of life
taking its course
striving against all odds

Suddenly,
unexpectedly
a fall, steep and frightening
love crashes down erratically
improbable to survive as one
then through a misty fog,
peace

The love gathers,
all the while expanding,
and is greater than before

Hannah Margrit Feil
Visalia, CA

Blessed

My biggest failure is my greatest asset
In the words of a true mindset, I have dreams
They take me sky high
I don't need the regular smoke a blunt to feel high
I'm settled even though life is hard
We can all win that gold metal
Replace my old thoughts, grind pushing me forward
Tumble over the top, provide a soft catch
I throw my ego hard at my peers
They know pressure, I tell them don't feel anxiety
Be the one in the spot light, step your game up
Hold your mic right, I promise you'll make it
You'll be there one day, people portray you in a certain way
People will betray you it'll be okay
Just stand up strong, take their judgement like a knife
Rip that knife out, slice the ones saying you'll never make it
Tell them god has never forsaken me, it was meant to be
Make sense of the money, life is a brand we all represent
Choose the right hands, you'll receive your blessings
Humble your power, know it's worth
Dive deep into your mind, caress your thoughts
Show the world what you're about, what you're striving for
Open doors to success, your life will never be a mess
You'll feel blessed

Trevor James Robinson
Forest City, NC

Broken

Shattered glass of a broken dream.
 A beginning; an end. No in-between.
 The blurred vision of indecision.
 Pieces of a puzzle that never quite fit.
 And the confusion... the confusion surrounding it.

Sindy Rowland
Dewitt, AR

The Wolf in the Wind

The East Mountain winds blow hard through the canyon
And clouds spill over the Sandias with abandon
'Til the cold settles in like ice on the valley floor
And the wind is howling like a wolf at your door

Now a stark moon is rising where the sun was obscured
Stealing what little warmth the clouds had secured
Let the moon and the wolf hold the night in their sway
For they both must yield to the new light of day

Thom Caruso
Albuquerque, NM

Ugly

He sat in front of his bedroom mirror,
And thought how someone could be so hideous.
How someone so repulsive could continue with daily routines.
How someone could look so tired,
yet sleep for scary extended periods of time with no dreams.
How someone could still talk and walk normally without being seen.
"How I could just still not be me"
He said, he thought in his head.
Words begin to slip in and out,
What's real what's not his heart going through a drought.
Insanity taking over and controlling his whole body—
all because someone began to call him ugly.

Izzy K. Torres
Houston, TX

Cowboy Hat

Watching a movie on my daddy's lap.
I said who's that guy in that cowboy hat.
That's John Wayne a matter of fact. I want to be just like that.
As I got older a cowboy hat wasn't cool.
When I wore it they stated I looked like a fool.
I moved to the city where people are strange.
They made me feel different and forced me to change.
A turned-around baseball cap seemed a better fit.
Turned to the side just a little bit.
Then one day I went to visit my hometown.
I tried to fit in but felt like a clown.
In the heartland where I grew up,
It's where you learn morals and manners when your a pup.
Everywhere I went people wore cowboy hats.
I remembered why I wanted to be just like that.
The kids all say "Yes mam, no sir" whey they talk to you.
The old people always smile and say"How do you do?"
There is a sense of pride from the people that live there.
They help each other out and really seem to care.
That cowboy hat is a passed-down tradition.
You can wear one but there are a few conditions.
Wear it proud and treat people fair.
If you have what someone needs be sure and share.
Always treat your elders with respect.
Be nice to those who serve and protect.
Take it off at the table and in church.
To get one's respect you won't have to search.
The next time you see someone in a cowboy hat,
Shake their hand and tell them thanks for being like that.

Colonel Kevin Gilbert
Parker, AZ

Dagger of a Broken Heart

Like a dagger my heart will stab
As it remains as broken glass
Sadly it won't retain the warm color of brass
Memories fade as they try to last
But yet for you, I was always last
Like the dagger my heart is stabbed
As you work in your playish lab
With all the girls that think they have the fab
You lost them However you always came running back
But this isn't where you can run a track so you lack
But like always you messed up
By trying to kiss up
Just do me a favor and just give up
The cops are involved
Your love for me dissolved
But I had no choice
I was your prey that you took by force
I just want to be free
Only if you can see how bad you hurt me
Now all I have left is my scab
From my daggered heart that was stabbed.

Ashley Elizabeth Cooper
Lakewood, CO

That Dark Hand

That dark hand is knocking on my door.
It's hard to keep that door closed
With a broken lock, but it wasn't like that before.
It has hurt me too many times in here.
It likes when I'm scared.
It knows I'm there, sitting in fear.

One day things will get better
One day everything will be alright.
The day I open that door
The light will be shining bright.

That dark hand is on my shoulder
But it made the mistake of looking back.
It was only for a quick second
But now I'm ready to attack.

Celeste Ponce
Los Angeles, CA

Pompus

An ember in the dark, is the simplest guide home.
As it glows in the night it must be mine. It is my inheritance.
Given from this blackened world around,
which so curiously continues to fail my needs.
As now that fire is within my grasp,
it will be fanned and made a flame.
Dancing its light across the valleys and ridges,
showing only I the way.
It should be grateful for its existence,
before I, what was it.
Now blazing full glory. The entire ethereal realm before me.
Pure white heat raging.
Brighter than the nearest star.
The peak of vision.
Simply to surprise this meager gift from a world so unworthy,
begins to fade.
Coiling back into itself,
a mere minor speck of red in an endless void.
Suffocated.
Along I go, to find a worthy ember.

Casey Goehl
Buena Vista, CO

Thoughts

I can hear you thinking
Daydreams and solitudes gone
Songs and heart strings fleeing
All except me belong

I can hear you thinking
Steps racing on by
Those served with grace
Hearing your song with mine

I can hear you thinking
Trapped on long wind's flow
A simple hope of seeking
Boldness in my old soul

I can hear you thinking
Giving away your smile
A million miles I'd run
To be your song in time

Booker McDowell
Spartanburg, SC

Too Hard to Understand

As kids we are told we can be Anything,
We will support you
is what they say
With standards hidden away

As long as they approve
Not me
But you

What do you mean?
May I not choose my destiny
My future, my fate, my inevitability

I just need your support
I don't need you to understand
For only I know

Who I am

My thoughts, my dreams
My hopes, my reasons

It is to hard to for you to understand
For only I know
Who I am

Wael Ahmad
North Bergen, NJ

Glass

Like broken glass, my remnants are fragile.
I am trying to piece myself back together.
Some pieces just don't fit the way they used to.
Every time I break I come back a bit different than the time before.
Sometimes better.
Sometimes duller.
But, I will always piece myself together,
No matter how many times you try to smash me into a million pieces.

Jocelyn Vizcarra
Norwalk, CA

Feelings Afloat

Submerged in the depths of nostalgia
Vanished into the abyss
Sunken by selfishness.
Wrapped by dark blue matter—
An off-white dress lingers.
Flashes of light flutter.
Near the bottom cold floor,
Whispers sealed in a glass bottle.
Tears shed like oil in the water,
A sweet escape, floating upward.
Yet I descend deep into the Mariana Trench.

Gustavo Munguia Jr.
Reseda, CA

The End

A delicate hand,
Tiny and tanned,
Sits atop her mother's mother;
Softer than the other.

As her time passes,
Waning without seeing the grass's,
True color or light;
Oh, the things she misses without sight.

Her body lay crumpled
Upon the bed without the slightest of delight,
And when she opened her mouth to speak,
You know her time couldn't have been tweaked.

As her eyes faded in the light,
And her hand lay limp at her side,
You know that she had been on quite a ride;
But now she has truly passed without a fight.

Xavier Sanchez
Freehold, NJ

Life

It is the most precious thing on earth
When she gave you that awesome birth
She loved you and gave you worth
She gave you life to live on earth.

She taught you how to live and love
That is why your thoughts are above
When your mother understood
When she raised you in the hood.

Mom and Dad showed you the way
Now you must know how to play
Molded in the way of clay
Now you must obey!

Life is short and will not last
So hope you think of your past
A good name is better, at last.

Chuck J. Glass
East Hampton, NY

Untold

As slaves of darkness, we are blinded.
We are fooled and lie in mockery,
Rudimentary facets unlike our own.
Ridiculed by the prospect of something more,
Something better than who we are.
And who are we? No one, nothing.
The world deems we have no importance, our cries are never heard.
They're snuffed out by the shadow we linger in
And there's no hope of stepping into the light.
There is no hope of rising above because in reality,
The weak never seem to ascend.
We shall not rise.
Not until there is no ground,
No foundation to break everything we've built.
The world is cruel and society has a way of stealing innocence
And stomping out the smallest iridescent light,
Leaving it broken and bloodied to revel in it's past blunder.
But we must be strong.
Strength is neither bequeathed nor acceded.
It is cultivated and fostered by the inexorable
Who extol the sorrows of men.
Who vaunt of engendered anguish.
Who pilfer and pillage our happiness
Until the husks that are reflected are the only selves we know.
We must be strong, have faith, and know pain.
Because no true happiness has ever known rendition.

Olivia Johnson
Amityville, NY

Tempest

The waves swirl and sweep,
They curl in the vast deep.
But the sailor knows not quit
As the thunder recedes not a bit.
This dedication and constant striving
Is but a part of his deep opining
To once again let his feet hold firm
On the solidity of a green berm.
No matter the dangers and the trials he avails,
The sailor hopes in naught but to quit the sail.
Yet when once his tongue tastes the ground,
His thirst for the vast blue is found.

Jason Dickey
Bowling Green, KY

Sea of Emotions

These waves of emotions constantly roll over me,
like waves in a storm, pulling me under,
holding me down.
My pleas, mere bubbles in this thick sea,
bursting before they even hit the surface.
Mixture of fear and sorrow creep around me,
pulling me deeper and deeper down.
Will I ever make it to the surface?
Or will I drown in these god forsaken emotions?

Rebekah Ramsey
Lincolnton, NC

Turbid Minds & Splintered Hearts

You can feel them. Their souls pouring into your mind like the sands in an hourglass. Your time is running out, or maybe it's just running Free. Wanting to be set loose you wait. Mind wandering with thoughts of love and wishing to feel such love that once encased you. The love that once brought you the happiness you longed for...

And as you sit here and wait, you don't know what you want, you don't know if you should hate. You tell them you're fine, but what's fine is the line that's reeling you in to the hope that you once had. That line is breaking, if it has been broken then you will be lost forever. A vicious reality that you wish to escape from. But, maybe you should cut that line, because you feel like you don't belong here and you are still running out of time... And hope...
You miss the things that you used to love, that you used to hold. Things that you never thought you'd miss the most. But you do, and you can't help it now as the darkness draws you in, as it begins to consume you. You find now that you can't breathe, the breaths you used to take with ease are now choking you. Like the smoke from a wildfire. Your lungs, they burn from the black fumes that are closing in. Your eyes fill with tears as you start to collapse, looking up you hope this pain will no longer last. But it does, and as you look at the sky you are filled with peace. The smoke begins to clear, slowly opening up the sky. The stars are near. Those bright beams of light bring you slowly back to life. Tears, they still stream down your black powdered face, making trails.
Your path to freedom. Your path to a new life...

Vienna Gonzales
Clermont, FL

We Shall Overcome

Pain, pain floods my memory.
It's time to take charge,
It's time for us to be free.
We march, we sing.
But darkness falls over us,
Dogs come to bite us.
We get sprayed with the water from the hose that's used to hurt us.
Children are put in jail.
But the police weaken.
I hear freedom in the air.
We shall overcome.

Poppy Elizebeth Beiser
Chicago, IL

Black Man Lost Child

I am a warrior,
A provider, a protector
Who'll snatch at your neck,
Break your chain of neglect,

Holding your golden jewels
In my hand with regret
As I recollect the victims
of unprotected sex.

Robert Emerson
South Bend, IN

Sorry

I wrote your name upon a foggy window
becuase I missed you.
I told myself that I'd be fine,
and that you were coming back.
The rain outside poured down,
like a river,
like the tears on my face.
And now I'm sorry that I left you today.

And now I'm alone.
I'm feeling so alone.
I have nowhere to call home.
Even though I'm already there.
Because I'm alone,
I'm feeling alone.

I thought that things would be better
if you left.
But now i realize that I was wrong;
things are so much worse.
And the rain outside poured down,
like a river,
like the tears on my face.
And now I'm sorry that I left you today.

Gabriela Rivas
Phoenix, AZ

My Path

I've chosen a path
that I call my own,
It leads me through life
and it leads me home.
It's a comfortable path
and it suits me well,
There's nothing to hide
no secrets to tell.
This path I walk
is like an old friend,
There is no beginning
and there is no end.
I am a part of it
and it is a part of me,
My never-ending path
that sets me free.

Barb Denny
St. Charles, MO

The Light

It is coming
Don't let it near
Legs numbing
Heart throbbing
Mind racing
Can't stop
Won't stop
Screams of pain
Darkness
Light from above
Flapping of wings
Glorious music
This is truly He
The Savior
The Hero
He has come

Mel Adams
Mt Juliet, TN

Five-Hundred Miles

Five-hundred miles it took me to arrive.
Your smile was worthwhile,
Straight from our love I do derive.

All the memories that I deprive
Make that beautiful smile turn vile.
Five-hundred miles it took me to arrive.

Your presence is all that I strive,
Even though you have been guile.
Straight from our love I do derive.

I have no clue how I continue to survive
When our love goes on trial.
Five-hundred miles it took me to arrive.

The start was as magical as a swan dive,
But now we have turned back the dial.
Straight from our love I do derive.

Our love is still alive,
We are becoming less hostile.
Five-hundred miles it took me to arrive.
Straight from our love I do derive

Shelbie Eklund
Castleton, IL

Chameleon

Too fat, no thigh gap,
Broad shoulders, no curves,
Thin lips, scattered freckles,
They gossiped.

So
Donned an appearance,
Like the judges around.
Wore crop tops, bikinis,
Pretended a smile.

Concealed dark circles,
Foundation for light skin,
Temporary beauty
Masking her scars.

Heard lies
And driven insane,
Artificial perfection lay
Hiding the same soul.

Fake
Like a plastic bottle,
Like a chameleon
Who cloaked
Her true colors.

Lauryn Wu
McLean, VA

Fall to Love

I fell to you in the dark, I fell to you in the light.
Now I fall to you in darkness, because I fear falling alone.
I fell to you because I hope you will catch me and hold me tight.
I fall to a love I shared with you, Hoping to feel it again,
the warmth of your love.
The warmth of the wolf that loves me.
that's my fall.... my fall for you.

Jessica Moore
Phelan, CA

Understanding

Yelling and screaming
Sounds of world war three
It's the storm before the peace
and I don't quite know how to make it
I conqueror one wave and another one knocks me over
I stand there with salty tears running down my face
The yelling won't stop and I...
I can't make it.
Me, no I'm not strong enough
but you, God you fought harder than anyone I ever knew
I didn't want to fight you
No, I wanted understanding

Cynthia Delores Biggs
Joshua, TX

A Prayer Away

Although I can't be near you
You cannot hear my voice
My hugs I used to give to you
Are memories in your thoughts
The way we used to laugh
The times we used to play
Seemed like only yesterday
My how fast time pass
There may be times you cry for me
Even times where you'll feel down
Just look up to the heavens above
And know I'm smiling down
When the day becomes too hard to bare
And you wish that you could call
Close your eyes and bow your head
Know that I'm only a prayer away

Diamantina Browdy
Houston, TX

Colorless

You can put a quote in a book,
It'll become a place you'll never look
In life we struggle day by day

We deal with our issues in our own separate way
We make mistakes and never let go
The emotions we feel, we just don't show—
Anger, hatred, sadness and spite
Emotions we feel when we think we are right
The grass so green and the sky so blue
Of the colors of the rainbow, these are two

Red
Orange
Yellow
Green
Blue

The end of the rainbow is all up to you
The way you see life, from your head to your toes
If you keep it inside, then no one ever knows
So grab a paintbrush and a canvas too
And draw the colors you see within you

There are challenges in life we don't want to face
We're in it together, we're in the same race
It's easy to give up and never look back
Take all your things, and just start to pack
But feeling like life is never really fair,
Well that's a feeling we seem to share.

Cori Hoberman
Hewlett, NY

The Orchestra Practice

The cello pierces the air with their short breath of notes.
It pulses, it's the heart of the orchestra.
Gently, the violas create a rhythmic harmony.
They are the legs and arms that dance to the music.
Slowly, the violin basks the sound with a whisper,
but soon it ebbs and flows till it sings a melody.
Each touch of the string creates clarion notes
that glide through the air like golden birds flying in the sunset,
and chords that gently fall down a musical waterfall.
Each attack of the bow, and caress of the string,
touch your imagination.
A march evokes majestic mountains and the shrill cries of war.
A light symphony creates sprawling verdant hills,
dotted with crystal dew drops.
The angry overture displays a ravenous sea,
clashing with the orders of the milky white moon.
A requiem sends a silvery drop of liquid down our eyes.
Yet, the heart beats of the cello, and the arms of the viola
allow you to escape the siren induced memories
and imagination of the violins.
They deeply connect you with the music, so that soon,
the cello's heart is your heart.
The violas' limbs are your limbs.
The Sweet voice of the violins
escapes your lips.
And you are one with the music.

Maya D. Nalawade
Darien, CT

Erisel Lord of Everlasting Night

Erisel, Lord of Everlasting Night
Won't you come and whisk me away?
Please take me into your domain
To live in the darkness among the creatures you rule.
This world of mine slowly drives me insane.
Demons run rampant, disguised as humans,
Tainting the innocent and causing chaos.
They say in your world, there is an absolute peace
Despite the dark gloom that shadows all.
Your lands are said to be free of bloodshed,
A place of beautiful, dark purity.
In this world, there is hardly a place
Where innocent blood was not wrongfully spilled.
I beg of you, my Lord Erisel,
Please take me away from this horrible place,
And bring me to your kingdom,
Where demons and humans can live as one,
Please, my lord, take me away from this hell,
And bring me to your kingdom,
Into a dark, but honest, peace.

Mikayla Edens
Irving, TX

Alchemist

Only true love can create an alchemist,
Heart of gold.
Transcending self,
Love becomes all that exists.

His existence becomes a manifestation
Of his every thought.
He creates his own reality,
Working through universal laws.

He spreads the blue flame of unconditional love,
Burning through the darkness of false realities.
This is where he finds perfection in everything
As only peace surrounds him.
This is
Bliss...

Marty Dustin Ulbrich
Studio City, CA

My poetry is about my personal revolution/evolution/awakening/realization that I can be everything I choose to be. I can literally change the chemistry in my brain with the thoughts I create. That destiny is only the seeds, which are planted in my conciseness by the environment I have been surrounded by. Fulfilling them only depends on my desire and will to diligently water them as they fruit dreams that could not possibly be imagined before. I passionately began to write poetry in 2012 after my first manic episode where I was diagnosed with bipolar disorder.

Forgetting to Remember

Walking without any idea where you're going
No idea who you're talking to
Or any idea who you are.
Something that you promised yourself that you would never forget,
Gone forever.
No knowledge that the one you loved so dearly,
That you built a family with, has passed.
Asking questions over and over again with no clue you are doing it.
The words that come out of your mouth not making sense to anyone
Other than you.
Laughing one minute and then crying the next.
Making people laugh, making people cry.
Thinking the one you admire so much, was just there visiting you.
No memories. No regrets.
No knowledge that you're sick with an illness that has no cure.
No knowledge that people can do nothing about it.
Whether you are by yourself listening through the walls
Or visiting in person, you don't know that you will soon forget it.
Some things you hardly remember, but still bring up maybe because
They bring you joy or maybe because
They bring you comfort.
No one really knows.
You may forget me, but I won't forget you!
I wish that I could turn back time, that this had never happened.

Bella Rossborough
Kennebunk, ME

Poem for the Hurting

It makes many people grimace,
how obsessed I am with my image.
How I am perceived by the world.
Its all in my written word.

Before I met you, I was just another,
one of many with one problem or other.
but with your gentle coaxing,
I grew tired of my hoaxing.

And with the faith you had in me, the flames of hate you smothered.

You don't deserve what's happened.
And our future is now fastened.
I'm ashamed to let you know,
and add to the long road you hoe.

Instead of sticking by your side, I've kept myself distracted.

JoBeth Eddings
Marquez, TX

Worn Down

The soles of my shoes
Are worn down, old, useless
Yet still I use them

Janset Aksoy
Auburn, AL

Depths of the Sea

He is from the depths of the sea
Treasures and gold illuminate
From above no one is able to see
Down below the waters suffocate
The sand is what covers his body
While creatures inhabit his soul
Days passed by while he disembodies
Dying by the treasure he stole
Took it from the ship he sailed
All hands on deck taking on water
The storm came in, mast had failed
Deck was gone, the storm was a slaughter
He came from the depths of the sea
Is he coming for you or me

Luke Dean Claiser
Elkton, MD

Crying to Myself

Crying to myself
I try to fall asleep,
Afraid to give in,
Nightmares slowly creep.
Dreams of slowly dying
Or sometimes super quick,
Giving in to the devil
I feel his forked tongue flick.
My nightmares are my weakness;
I can never win.
My past will always haunt me,
Reminding of every sin.
I am so very tired;
All I want is rest,
But with sleep comes the visions—
The things that I detest.
I am getting weary,
So very scared of the dark.
What's to come of me tomorrow
When the sun's heat has spark?
Will I be okay?
Will I get through this pain?
Do I have to swallow it,
And go through it all again?
I try to relax
And lay down for the night,
But comfort will never find me
For I'm always full of fright.

Margaret Bravo
Omaha, NE

Thunderclap

I spent our days in contentment
And knew not of the storms waged within you
Of the wild rains pouring down your cheek
Hidden from me so you didn't seem weak
In my moment of nostalgia
In remembrance and retrospect
I turned my gaze back, to the aftermath
Of my raging winds which razed our path
They then dealt unto me a tumultuous blow
The thunderous chord of an all time low
Inhale, exhale
Our silent breaths once in tandem
Like one mind now torn apart
With broken shallow breath I utter
Be still, be still my beating heart

Anthony Dyllan Kimbrell
Florence, AL

No One Understands

Sometimes things don't go as planned,
You feel left in the dirt, lost, with no one to run to.
You feel like no one understands what you're going through.
You feel as if even if you do tell someone about what's going on,
Their going to judge you or may just think it's for attention.
Walking with your head down every day
Witnessing opinions and it constantly hurts you.
Going home praying that the next day will be better
But it gets worse.
No friends so your calm about everything but you're mentally fed up.
Turning to people that you expect to understand
And say they will always be there but give up on you.
You look for little ways to get out of things
Not realizing how large the situation that you're in .
Sometimes you overreact not meaning to,
But to show people that you're okay.
Your doing stuff to fit in with your friends but go home to drama.
Entering and leaving out of school,
scared no one hurts you to your next destination.
Making hard decisions looking for the better outcome in yourself.
Somethings just get harder by the day and you get lost.
Listening to music that makes you think.
Living your life off of facebook and instagram quotes.
Worried about how many likes your getting on a picture,
Rather than how many points you can get on a test.
Everyone has a story,it takes only them to understand.
No one will understand.

Destiny Antoinette Arnold
Chicago, IL

Four-fifths

The taste is sweet
His touch, soothing
The smell, soft
His sound is harmony
But his sight is sour

I've been dancing with the devil
As beautiful as it is perceived
As graceful as I move
My security is lost

The conscious decision of my actions
The constant need for reassurance
He wraps his arms around me as I reach for comfort
Epiphanies glow in the in the darkness of his eyes

I've been dancing with the devil

In the facade of his arms
My happiness strengthens
His warmth cools
Finding peace within myself
Loving each sensation
I become my whole

Molly Ann Smith
Highland, CA

Father

On his death bed,
"I'll be a better father," he said.

I tried smiling through the tears.
Could he really change after all these years?

The late night, eight-hour drive
Gave me time to reflect on life.

Still young and accustomed to his lies,
I cautiously believed the love in his eyes.

There was nothing I wanted more
Than to have him show is love, unlike before.

A miracle it was that he lived,
And all these years later, I continue to forgive.

I've had two daughters since that day.
"We do not know him," they would say.

A better father he did not become.
I'm so thankful I have a different one.

My true Father is God alone.
This earth is not my forever home.

Amber Yokum
League City, TX

God's Earth

Time seems to go in slow motion
When I'm staring at a blue ocean
Or a still, unmoving sky.
Cars are nonexistent and money
is a figment of the imagination
There is no such thing as a country or a nation.
The only things that are relevant
Are the leaves whispering a wild, sweet sentiment
In my yearning ear.
The sleeping grass and the leaning tree,
The quick squirrel pausing to gaze at me.
Air is thinner, cleaner, better
And suddenly I am a queen in her homeland,
Made to be agile—run, kick, stand.
My veins pulse with the thick blood of the forest
And my lungs of bone are laced with a grassy vine.
My legs are long and lean,
strong as the bark of the trees
And my voice is smooth but powerful,
as the nature speaks through me.
My footsteps echo across a solid earth
While I breathe in, soak up, gulp down
Everything that the Earth has to offer me.
To offer us.

Cassie Herring
Manassas, VA

We Are the Teenagers

Eyes are dripping
Grades are slipping
The bathroom door tightly shut
Skin is cut
Arms bleeding red
Thoughts spill from our heads
Finding no one's our friends
Knowing this isn't normal
We quit being formal
You say we are strange
So we try to change
But in the end
All we want is life to end
We get called reckless
But your past isn't messless
You blame society for how we act
But let's not forget who did the parenting act
We are the teenagers who you over look
Scared we'll mess up your perfect book
We'll do just that
If our stomachs aren't flat
Or if we don't have a thigh gap
So Yes,
Eyes are dripping
Grades are slipping
The bathroom door tightly shut
Skin is cut
Arms bleed red
We can't get your words out of our heads

Lindsay Martin
Garden Plain, KS

Time

Thief, thief, thief, greatest of thieves
You stole my boy
You took my heart and my life from me
Unbounding, unmerciful, deceptive, and cunning
Oh sweet fool, greatest of thieves
Time announces its effort when victory rears
Time announces its strength when failure appears

Unbounding, unmerciful, deceptive, and cunning
Oh sweet fool, greatest of thieves
Time it hides before,beyond, beneath
It hinders, it hurries, running, running abroad
Behind the shadows, oh greatest of thieves

Justice if it be or not makes no deals (like it or not)
The thief ever present ever past
When the wind blows—when the sun shines
When it rains—when it snows
When the sun sets—when the sun rises

Oh greatest of thieves
If I could just have a little more time
If I could just of had a little more sense
Fate...Inevitably God is always in control
And free Will...God take the wheel

Maria Louise Mingarelli
Aubrey, TX

Hope

I wake up, and you're still there like a nagging unwanted guest.
I rollover off the bed unable to push myself up,
getting ready to embrace yet another day with pain by my side.
My invisible illness felt like a dirty secret
that I had to conceal from the world.

I began going down the dark unending road, questioning: why me?
Will I ever get my life back?
Will anyone ever love someone in this condition?
This path was neither productive nor beneficial to my recovery.
I figured what did I possibly have to lose
if I at least tried my best,
and I clung onto that belief like a mother protecting her child.

I pushed through every day practicing my warrior spirit,
believing there is always hope that it will get better.
Just as I began to accept myself for whom
I was at that point in time—
It eventually did get better, physically and emotionally.

Believing in hope, and eventually myself, is what got me there.
My unwanted guest may still rear its ugly head in varying degrees,
but I'm no longer worried, because I have hope...
Hope in myself and better days to come.

Lauren Donnelly
Cambridge, MA

My Child

I hear your voice my child
I hear your cries at night
I feel your sorrows
I see your tears
Welling up in your eyes
Your cries carry out in the darkness
I want the pain to leave you
I lay in my bed and cry
I cry because I am weak
I cannot stop the pain from swallowing you
I know every time you take a breath
Life slowly leaves you
I wish
My God I wish
I could make it stop
But I can't
Oh my child
I'm sorry for the pain
For the sorrow
The torture brought upon you
Please forgive me
My Child.

Jo Furious
Compton, CA

Deep Inside the Universe

Deep inside the universe lies a teardrop.
Deep inside that teardrop, there I am.
So as rivers overflow
And seas run dry,
There I be, still alive.

Draped in loneliness, yet naked in fear.
My soul will dwindle, year by year.
The moon holds my secrets;
My hopes rest upon the sun.
In a box high on a shelf lies my sanity
So that I may never come undone.

In a sacred pact, forever with him
For making me be, I am never to sin.
Destiny twinkles in the dark
In a galaxy far away.
While a girl lies underneath, dreaming of better days.

Although not together
Divided we are never.
Maybe through a wormhole
I will find you and me
In a parallel world
Where anything may be.

Cheryl George
Rutland, VT

A Normal Day

It was a normal day I woke up to see,
The sun shining brightly through the trees,
Oh! What a day it will be!

There was a big dip,
The four wheeler flipped,
We only wish the rope had ripped.

His heart was gold,
We wished we were old,
Many wise stories he could have told.

The ambulance came,
We knew things wouldn't be the same,
R.I.P River you were the only one that kept us sane.

Kylie Beth Tempelmeyer
Fort Smith, AR

Mother's Love

What is love, but the vigorous emotion
from the depths of our heart?
What is unconditional love? A mother's love
that will never forsake her children in
the wickedness of this world.
How can anyone ever compare to a
mother's love that is eternal?
A love that will never leave,
but stays by her children's side.
Even in the darkest hours of life
she is there.
Even when the world turns its back
and forsakes you
she is there.
When the pain is so cutting
she is there.
Even in her darkest hour she is there
with open arms to take her children's pain.
How then can any man fathom a mother's love?
Love that suffer for the good of her children.
How can her children, imagine this love?
We can't, but what we all know
is this: you're 50 and we're not.
Happy 50th Birthday, Mom

Melinda Baker
Jacksonville, FL

A Story for Future Pieces

No two pieces are quite the same,
A different position each has to claim.
So different these pieces are in fact,
No corners the same, no colors exact.

Some are pieces not so new,
Where they belong, they have a clue.
Reuniting with whom they please,
Reminiscing old memories.

Newer pieces, lost in oblivion,
Knowing not the place they are meant to be fitting in.
Questioning their personalities,
To cope, some develop a safe reality.
Living in fields of hopes and dreams,
A bunch of abstract sketches of faint future gleams,
Each pretending to be dancing glass figurines,
Under blue moonlight and shining streams.

But they'll realize that among their dream,
They all share a common theme.
Differences need not change their way,
Each will define where they fit one day—
Possibly with a little help to find their place,
To together, create the world's bright new face.

Lori Eng
New York City, NY

School Blues

We find disappointment in ourselves
Like long lost toys behind dressers
In school we find ourselves physically present but mentally absent
Depression at an all time high happiness at an all time low
Stress is the reason why we drop out
Dropping out of windows is our answer
We are killing ourselves over numbers
We go to school do something equivalent to our best
But yet it still isn't enough
How come what I see good in my head doesn't meet your marks
We pretend to not be phased by every low grade
But slowly it tears us down brick by brick until
we have nothing left shielding our motivation
After school we are left with fractions of ourselves
We will never be whole again
We are told to aim high to achieve greatness
how can we even do our best
when we don't even have motivation to live
We are asked by teachers to reflect on what we did
What are we most proud of, nothing
What we could have did better, everything
What if our doing better is not waking up that morning of
Or hurting ourselves because you know inside
that your best will never measure up
We are told that grades don't make you
But they sure do break you

Erika Price
Philadelphia, PA

Daddy's Medicine

My Mommy said, "Bath time, Boy Blue!"
My Mommy said, "Wash your butt!"
My Mommy said, "I'll be back, my Blue."
I sitted in the tub forever.
Water's freezing like ice now. No more bubbles.
My toes are mushy raisins. No towel.

"Ma!"
"Ma!!"
No Ma.

My Daddy fastly come in and looks mad and sweaty.
My Daddy fastly shutted the shower curtain.
My Daddy fastly said,"Don't look, chamaco!"
I looked in the itty bitty rip in the itty bitty rip in the curtain.
He put a scary needle in his arm. Must be Daddy's medicine.
Daddy's medicine is always like really ugly, dirty water.
He lays back on the the toilet.
He closes his brown eyes.
He looks happy now. Still sweating.
He moves a little.
He shakes a lot.
He falled hard. He shakes more.

"Ma!!!"
"Ma!!"
"Ma!"

No Ma.

Bernie Toledo
Chula Vista, CA

Carmen

You're the prettiest woman I know
Your smile is best made of sunshine and snow
Your hair was shining your movement a grace
When you turned to me I gazed at your beautiful face

Can you hear the truth you have spoken
By not giving your heart up that could be broken
You could talk with people and keep your virtue
Stick with me and nobody will ever hurt you

In my eyes and heart you can do no wrong
My feelings for you are very strong
If you just give me a chance to show you
I promise you will never feel sad or blue

Jason B. Johnson
Cairo, GA

From Silence to Salvation

Just living this thing we call life can be agony
Expect adversaries around each and every corner
Strength always being given to the unworthy from the wicked
Upon us all evils seem to fall
Sunrise never quite arrives

Supernaturally turbulent nights abound, tribulations do not cease
Aligned with us others stand
Voices crying never to be heard—each cornered to the
End of a plank where we find ourselves trapped—left to suffer in a
Silence so loud it ruptures eardrums

Through it all we look closer
Closer at a message we cannot forget
We are not the last but the first
Like first words
Just expect strength upon sunrise
Supernaturally aligned voices end silence
And first letters
Jesus saves

Evangelyne Dillice Eliason
Aurora, CO

A Human Breeze

I want to disappear into a thousand microscopic pieces.
To live amongst the echoes and raindrops where things collide,
but they're always cohesive. Nothing would be constant;
it would change slower than eroding sandstone;
my very existence would depend on if you accept the unknown.
The options would be endless though the decisions simple.
Simply existing would be a decision in itself
to allow the wind to carry me from town to town
to interact with the word, but visibly alone.

Though maybe that's the problem.
The contradiction that keeps us whole.
A need to be personally acknowledged in a way a summer breeze
cannot.
Except the breeze can never be branded with fingerprint opinions,
have expectations embroidered in its palms
or absorb worry quite like the human skin.
It doesn't have to have the answers to any of your questions,
except which way to face the sail.

Sometimes I wish I were the autumn wind.
The kind that dances with the falling colors and laughs at the rain.
The wind that says snow is on the way, but no one baits an eye.
Time would be my own and I for I.

Grace Virginia Carter
Black Mountain, NC

Swimming in Space

I wish I could
Swim in space.
I wish I could
be embraced in the
inky black sky.
I wish I could
feel the warmth of the stars
and glance at the galaxy's gems
face-to-face.
I wish I could
let my Earth weight fall away.
I wish I could
hear nothing but space's nature.
I wish I could
see a sliver of a silver shining moon.
I wish I could
swim in space,
but until that's possible,
I will stare into space's depths,
till I can swim in space.

Elizabeth Marie Clark
Austin, TX

Summer in Sequoia

Fire
A ravenous flame opens the way
Black smoke darkens a sunny day
A light so bright inspires such fear
The fire consumes all I hold dear
Her face reminded me of
    Fire
What stood so tall is now hollow inside
Blackened embers of that which has died
The stump on a cliff without a name
Tells of a force no one can tame
I heard her name but all I saw was
      Fire
Ethereal flowers surround as if from dreams
Majestic mountains with shimmering streams
Yet these are hardly worth a mention
The power of fire demands attention
Her eyes contained such
        Fire
Out of ash the tallest trees rise
Countless others meet their demise
The cone needs fire to touch the sky
Nothing is certain it can only try
Am I the ash or a seed given hope?
        Fire

Michael Parrish
Madison, WI

Split Relationship

Look I love your mom because she made you, baby
But she manipulates your mind in high hopes that you'll hate me
And her only defense is pretending I'm crazy
Look I only sold dope to buy you clothes from Macy's
With a nickel in my pocket I still gave you the best
Even when your mama left
I was dying inside but still I hid my stress
And your kisses proved to me I passed the God test
I know I've been bad, took you for granted again
But that doesn't reflect the type of father I am
All lies, you say you hate me but can't look in my eyes
She got a good stepdad but he's stealing my time
You tore my heart apart letting him have what's mine
You called child support to chase my last dime
I gave you one inch then you took a mile
You gave me one glimpse into hell with a smile

Joseph Antony Flores
Walla Walla, WA

The Best Man

All was silent but the sounds of harps and strings;
snowy wings and feathers flew as doves took the air.
Her hair and face covered with a transparent veil,
and the tail of her bridal dress was posh and pale.

We all stood in awe in muted ovation, amazed,
and praised her gracious glide toward the altar.
And I faltered at the sight of her smile
and style as she drifted down that radiant aisle.

I thought about when she and I had walked
and talked together in that lonely park
after dark, discussing our future plans.
My hands had reached for hers to hold and band.

I thought I'd be the one forever in her life,
until I watched her become my best friend's wife.

Dasheek King Dennis
Norcross, GA

Addiction

Sometimes I wonder if I can go on
Even if tomorrow comes
When the sun brings a new day
I pray I find my way
The path I'm on now is full of darkness
It's a road that gives with harshness
Full of demons around every corner
Waiting to watch me falter
Day after day and night after night
I'm always in a fight
I have more scars on the inside
Than I do the outside
This temporary feeling inside
A feeling that's really disguised
It draws me deep inside its grip
Only to let me go alone on this trip
By myself scared and frightened
Lost and unguided
My life as an addict
With my vision full of static
What I do today keeps me lost
I pray for tomorrow that I find my way

Jeremy Earl
Corryton, TN

I Am Doing Everything

I am doing everything I know to do
Nothing is going right, but what is new
Seems things never go my way
But that only makes me stronger today
I won't let life get to me
My head is held high can't you see
I pray to God that life gets better
Like I am doing now as I write these letters
My faith in God and my trust in you
Keeps my heart pure and our love so new
I hold your love close to my beating heart
My love for you will never part
You give me strength to keep moving ahead
Making the best of life, forward I tread
My love for you is all I have now
I don't need anything more and that I vow
To be honest, faithful, and love only you
That's my plan, that's my goal, not giving up, and always being true
I love you forever, baby
That's a definate, never a maybe

Cindy Denise Norman
Des Arc, AR

Chasing Happiness

Happiness is there
Often unrealized
We search and hunt for it
But it's right before our eyes

We search for it in wallets
And on Google too
But we come out empty-handed
Because it comes from within you

It is found in a hug
Or a welcoming smile
Though these gestures are simple
They are remembered for quite a while

Because these truly are the things
That bring happiness to the heart
And hugs and smiles,
Are but a mere start

Mariam Sarhan
Santa Clara, CA

Human

I'm optimistic.
I'm pessimistic.
I'm conservative.
I'm liberal.
I find warmth being basked in the light.
I find comfort being shrouded in the dark.
I desire the truth.
I lie to all.
I call for peace and equality.
I call for war and alienation.
I extend a hand to those in need.
I cut the rope of those who hold me back.
I know how to love.
I know how to hate.
I'm a one of kind, an original.
I'm the biggest copycat.
I'm the ace of spades.
I'm the two of hearts.
I'm the biggest gamble ever played.
I am the greatest creation ever made.
I am the biggest mistake to walk the Earth.
Who am I?
I am you.
You are me.
I am human.

Jordan Darkis
Hays, KS

One-Way Ticket

The one way ticket to Sadness
Is a journey that never goes back.
The moon sips the black tea of night,
Watching with wide, glowing eyes.
Perhaps the sun would not greet
Her halfway at the peak of their mountain.
Instead, she'd be frozen in the middle of
Her stars' never-ending ball, cursed to dance
Alone into the tunnel that runs through fate.
Ironically—as I am the moon, and you are the sun—
Your light seems to be incompetent to my dark.
My soul is void and cold, and yours so full of life—my life
Lives with yours, telling me that true happiness does exist;
And after all, I know this, for it only exists with you.
Don't follow me into the waters of fear and hate,
For your fire would only burn out, flirting with smoke
Stay as you are, loving the clouds instead of me; testing
How long they will remain in the sky with you.
Leave the moon to her parties where she's surrounded by love,
And yet remains so unloved and alone.
The one way ticket to Sadness is one that never returns,
And moreover, I only purchased one.

Katrina Ann Whitaker
North Las Vegas, NV

Flying Stones

It's flying,
Then gliding,
Across blue leather.
Skipping like kittens.

How many can you make?
1...2...3...4...
Hop
Hop
Hop
Splash!
Then it falls
Sinking deep into
The leather.
No more skips
It's time is up
It's time for a new stone to take it's place
And skip across blue leather.

Jasmine Faith Vidrine
Katy, TX

Love VS Anger

Anger,
When anger is in the air,
Your heart fills with despair.

Or your heart breaks,
That's all what it takes
To ruin love that could of gave you happiness.

When that love is all around,
Your heart starts to pound.

Or you sigh in belief,
With relief
That you will get happiness through the love.

Baily Ann Carpinelli
Denver, CO

Power to You

Brown skin girl there's nothing to be ashamed of.
The shades of your physique are more than unique.
The density of your hair turns heads.
Your brown eyes shine brighter than the golden sun.
They want to be like you, look like you, why not be proud?
Why not hold your fist full of pride beyond the skies.
Your black is more than beautiful, it's radiant.
It's yours, you own it.
There will be those who may try to bring you down.
There will be those who may hate.
There will be those to judge you.
And there will be those to test your fate.
But know this God makes no mistakes.
Being black is being bold, powerful, and strong.
Being black is beautuiful and beyond words to fully describe.
By being black you are destined for greatness and success.
By being black you're being blessed.

Krystal Murphy
Lancaster, CA

Love Me Slowly

Dear Lover,
Tonight, when you come home and tenderly kiss my forehead
Will you linger slightly longer?
Let your lips leave an imprint on my skin and on my soul

When you touch me
Allow your fingers to draw raining hearts on my belly
And write old fashioned love letters on my shoulders
Let them be a tool in loving me

But do not
Give time a chance, a turn, with our love
Push the numbers aside and slow down, against the tide
Let time fade, and love me slowly

Grace R. Roat
Watsontown, PA

The Path

I awoke one early morning, to fetch the food and drink;
a daily chore it was to me, plus, it gave me time to think.

So I set off into the wood, a pail in my hand,
upon the path I knew so well; a grassy indent in the land.

However, when I reached the path, my shoes so wet with dew,
I noticed that the path had split; now not one, but two.

So startled was I that I dropped my pail; my brain could not permit,
how in one day a single path, could simply, somehow, split.

And then I noticed another thing, a sign beside each trail;
one read "food" another "water"; either way was sure to fail.

For a person needs food as much as water, but yet I had to choose.
There was no time to take both trails; I would win only to lose.

So I slowly sat upon my pail, thinking only of the worst.
I could choose food and have a feast! Only then to die of thirst.

Of course I could yet take the other, and quench the thirst within.
Yet with no food I would not live; this path too, was not a win.

So if you wonder what path I chose, what's the answer to the tale...
I cannot say for I am still, sitting on my pail.

Stefanie Doran
San Antonio, TX

Today the Angels Sing

Today the angels sing,
for they have yet another
angel flying with them up in the summer skies.
I know that you are in a better place
now but that doesn't mean you won't
be missed down here.
Today the angels sing,
as they gave
you your wings and welcome you
to your new home; I wish I could
come visit you but Heaven is a
little far away.
Today the angels sing,
so I ask for one last little
thing if you don't mind: please
watch over our family—you know
how crazy we can be for you
know us all to well.

Amy Stone
Bloomsbury, NJ

El Capitan—Full Moon

Moonlit monolith
Climbers' lanterns flicker on your face
Like raucous fireflies

Below
Envy filled, entranced
We imagine such a night's rest
On your glacier-carved brow
Suspended by rope and piton in a hammock-cocoon
Sharing ledges with Eagles and Stellar Jays
To view grand Yosemite
Tenayas' Ahwanhee
As her valley's granite giants yawn
Eager for heavy sleep
While the Lunar Mother
Reaches beyond their shoulders
To ever-so-gently
Close our wondering eyes.

Rhonda Joyce Branum
Carbondale, IL

Untitled

I control you in such a way that it's scary.
I'm your master!
You listen to me more than your spiritual adviser or pastor.
Steal, kill, manipulate.
It's now in your character once you acquire a passion for me.
But you're blinded by the material things so you cannot see.
I'm a necessity in this world, you need me there's no debate.
Life without me wouldn't be so great.
Possessing me, I can give you the things that your heart desires.
Your flesh is appeased and sings with a sweet melody like a choir.
The bible refers to me as the root of all evil.
That's quite scary.
I'm capable of changing my image.
I can be your advocate or either your adversary.
The ones you love and adore get demoted,
on your priority list when it comes to me.
You even lose track of yourself, but your too in denial to see.
Name it! I'll give it to you.
House, cars, diamonds, silver and gold.
But in return I just want one thing,
and that's your very precious soul.

David Hollamon
Erie, PA

Who Am I?

I laugh at you as I dance around in your head, confusing your thoughts
I whisper in your ear and tell you "there's no reason to try"
I make you shake with fear when you think of taking a chance
I keep your darkest secrets then flash them in front of you
just when you think you have conquered them
I know your desires and make you feel ashamed of what pleases you

Who am I, you ask?
I am the one you gave control of your life
I am the one that's tired of playing this game
I am the one that is ready to see you fight back
I am the one that knows you are stronger then you think

My first name is fear; I answer to it proudly
My middle name is doubt; you're never sure when I'm around
My last name is shame; humiliation is my forte

Who Am I?

Tonya Michelle Washington
Sandston, VA

Liberty

Atop the cherry bricks of the state house in Philadelphia
Chiming incessantly against indigo skies,
She speaks.

Though,
A mishap
A mistake
A momentary lapse
Resulted in a glaring blemish that would remain.
Unfixed.

Inequality,
Division,
Hatred,
Corruption unfixed.

Yet, despite her obvious flaws I remain, fixated,
Appalled at her boldness,
Perplexed by her permanence,
And captivated by her beauty.

She is not perfect,
But she IS
And will be
For as long as she has breath.

So please, my fellow patriot, I implore you
let freedom ring.

Sanni Iyintosoluwa Haruna
Chicago, IL

Why Me

Burning hurt of salt in a wound
Why me
Blurring of my vision
Head swimming
I've got to make a final decision
Why me
I haven't done anything to deserve this
I only want to be loved
How did it get so twisted
If there was a beginning sign I missed it
Why me
Eyes wide open I walked into a wall
Battered and bruised with no one to cal
One eye open still trying to find my way
Walking in a fog
When will I find the day
Why me
Why me
You said you would die for me
Why me
You said you'd love me for always
Why me
Do I deserve this pain
Why me

Francine N. Moore
Poplar Bluff, MO

What My Eyelids Hide

I can't know what my eyelids hide,
   Masquerading did undermine.
It's no surprise the dog has died,
   At my table you came to dine.
Masquerading did undermine,
   Peel the pain layer by layer.
At my table you came to dine,
   Raise the sword, let drip you slayer!
Peel the pain layer by layer,
   Inside and out it's all the same.
Raise the sword, let drip you slayer,
   What I don't see won't smell of shame.
Inside and out it's all the same,
   It's no surprise the dog has died...
What I don't see won't smell of shame,
   I can't know what my eyelids hide.

Susan Ashley
Acushnet, MA

The Phoenix

Like a Phoenix she rose from the ashs.
And her was bright red like a flame.
And I can the fire in her eyes.
And I can see the passion deep inside.
As she lets out a battle cry.
And finally I can the love in her heart.

Daniel Lee Victorian
Ann Arbor, MI

Acceptance

Unwrap the next layer of this female individual
Her inner core is dark,
Bruised with hateful words
Yet her exterior beams
Full of life and warmth
She finds that those hardest to see
Are easiest to find
And those who blend in
Stand out
Yet she can't place herself in life
So she follows others
Hoping they lead her right

Luis Garcia
Brooklyn, NY

I Wonder

I wonder!
I wonder why it rains on me
I wonder how my life will be.
I wonder if my dreams will come true
And wonder why I haven't a clue.
I wonder if I will accomplish my goals
Or will they just settle like mold.
I wonder if they could see how my adult life would be.
I wonder if this is just a dream
Because should it be as hard as it seems.
I wonder when the pain will end
Wondering if it's because I've sinned.
I wonder why it rains on me
I wonder how my life would be.
I wonder why it is now
I wonder why it was then
Still wondering when will it end.

Kimberly Pyatt
Moncks Corner, SC

Dear Elestus

How is it that one simple choice, can ruin a life forever?
  The choice that you thought, you wouldn't make, ever.
When I made that decision, it felt wholly right,
  But the split second after, I began to live in eternal night.
When we made the choice—the choice to follow Lucifer,
  We were promised much power, and many would bow to us in turn.
But I found out very soon, that he not only lied to humans
  But to us as well; it was a language in which he was fluent.
Still though we were free and happy about that . . .
  We simply redirected our worship, to him it was pointed at.
I didn't care as long as it pleased me . . . what I did for him
  I didn't realize that we were really setting a foundation for sin.
I wanted to come home, I really did, my brother,
  But he wouldn't let me leave; he said we were bound to one another.
I begged and I pleaded for him to let me go
  But he said he couldn't—every time he said no.
Why didn't you stop me? You were right by my side,
  When I said I'd join them, you just stood by and cried.
I remember the feeling, that feeling of dread
  When I joined his dark forces and found myself dead.
My decision was permanent, oh I know that now;
  And I know coming home, Satan will never allow.
So I wish that you, Elestus my friend,
  Would tell Elohim for me, before I meet my end
That I'm sorry for my actions—I ruined what he gave—
  And I wish I could reverse this decision I made.

Grace Quigley
Golden City, MO

My Heart Is Like a Cave

My heart is like a Cave
Few dare enter only those who are brave
You may ask what is so bad but the dark
Scattered remains and a dog's hollow bark
My internal beast is scared of the light
Light brought from stranger's lacking sight
They can't see my past for the candle goes out
My pain and torment is the hollowing wind
They fear that they can't make it to the bend
Soon they are caught in the web beset by doubt
They stayed there added to my pasts remains
Bound by my mental, emotional chains
But the cave's treasure was around the bend
In the middle of my hollow heart den
Then the dog lets out a shallow howl
Followed by a painful growl
My heart is like a Grave

Jacob Nathaniel Thompson
Cedartown, GA

Apologies to a Broken Soul

How does one apologize to the shattered?
How does one say sorry to those it tore apart?
When mistakes are made, can one be forgiven?
When broken, how do you mend ones heart?
The tragedies that those have faced
Outweigh ideas we perceive.
From a foggy past to regret filled actions,
The pain is greater than we believe.
So how does one make up for things,
They should or should not have said?
Can words heal or maybe actions can end,
The victims eyes blinded by red?
Will they know you care?
Will they see sincerity?
Will they lash out or start a fight?
Will they see you there?
Will they know you're guilty?
Will anything make things right?
To you, the one who I've hurt so dear,
Is there anything more I can do?
Through thick and thin I'll stick around.
I'm here and I will always love you

Ender Christian Kongkaeow
Round Lake, IL

My Own Mind

I hate the expectations that
are held on people,
as if your idea
of being successful
is the same mind.
When morning comes relieved,
glad that the
insane person in
my head seems to vanish.
Most nights that voice
tells me to stay up and
think; after awhile
my insecurities cover
me up like a blanket
swallowing me
whole. Sometimes I think of
everyone as a super hero.

Cecelia Latrice Thigpen
Cahokia, IL

Angelic Descent

Love without calm purpose
Fulfilled to your heart's content
Something lost now has hope
It came from lost cover
A supreme event
A priority sent
Better left on its course
Love stole my heart anew
Something to run free, yes
But I should lose myself
Astray beyond heart's hope
Fear won't control our life
Breath fate into this heart
Hearts once lost and now found
Froze by hate and contempt
Love dies and soon comes back
Not to haunt, but be free
A blaze started from loss
Fed by the new kindle
Started by you rather
I get lost in your eyes
Brown eyes and dark skin
Beauty to gaze upon
A god amongst insects
Perfect in every way
I will never lose sight

Scott Anthony Hale
White Oak, TX

This Is My Home

This is my home, 'tis where I'll stay
Till all of time has passed away
'Twas here I lived, 'twas here I died
'Tis here always I will reside
Though some will come and others go
Through autumn leaves and winter snow
Through moonlit night and seasons change
The rest will go, yet I remain
For I am in the plaster walls
The sunny rooms and darkened halls
The attic gloom, and cellar must
The chimney soot, the curtains' dust
And when in bed at night you sleep
Within my room, beneath your sheets
'Tis I who touch your pillow case
And blow iced breath across your face
And watch you in the morning glow
And hear the things I shouldn't know
It's me who makes the silent moan
That makes you feel you're not alone
Within my house where I will stay
Until you've died and moved away

Michael Ross Valentine
Bellows Falls, VT

The Kingdom

Stop the marching, flaring, blaring sirens, double time
Quick the beat of drumming, humming further down the line
Passing torches over, under, burning brightly cinders blowing
Rise the tides of rushing waters healing sickly lands need flowing
Dusk and dawn no longer hinder thoughts of glowing in moonlight
Founding fathers bathe their children in the light of minds insight
Towards the shorelines all will enter tossing hats among the lanes
Further branching out their families intermingling natures plains
No more coin of yesterday's world shall a taker be ensnared
Bid a farewell to the need for nothing to be shared
Keep your hearts held closer to a kinder sort of man
Teach a fellow traveler how to hold a child's hand
Take upon yourselves now to throw a stone at none
Stricken down with costly consequence is the holder of the throne
Silent hope will flourish as driftwood comes to shore
Simple times give cause to tending fields of wheat implore
Mountains hold the echoes of a past with troubled time
Seas filled with the answers swallow whole the bitter rhyme
Tempted are the ones who stray among the greens of grass
Follow not the footsteps of an unbeaten sort of pass
Swipes of waves will wash away the line drawn in the sand
Skies of gray will empty and rid a dirty land
Somber faces look to rays of light above
Emerging clouds of solace pierced by a single dove
Golden is the Kingdom for those who hold it high
Never will you enter as mere a passerby

Tamara Horton
Melrose, MN

Drunken Tree

Freshly sober, and I am longing for the merciful crimson shade
of my drunken tree,
where under its protective umbrella the blurred clarity of false
reality blinds me in deceptive comforting shadows, and its thick
sticky fog of ignorance smoothers my pain,
as I lay there reading mine own Malleus Maleficarum for all that
that is wrong, with no such branches pointing at mine self, such
a thing would be heresy.
I start sinking into its thickness of contempt and rue, no longer
reaching out for reason or truths, playfully lost in numbness and
hazy foresight, suffocatingly dismal and trite.
And yet, beyond its shadows of utopic self loathing, I embrace and
welcome the novelty of this unfamiliar freshness and clearness.
A new day arises, and I shall bask in all its glory, with
anticipation and hunger for more to come.
One day I shall take an axe to it, my old friend, but for now
it sits solemnly on a lonely hill, in the middle of a
of a lonely field, in the middle of nowhere,
waiting for me.

Patrick Ah-Wong
Orlando, FL

The Songbirds

A songbird of blue sung high in the trees
And filled the spring air with her own melodies.
She was content with no care for a mate
Until she heard a sound that changed her fate.

There was another songbird who was singing her song
So she went out to find her while humming along.
The two songbirds met and they instantly knew,
Like flowers in spring, so their love grew.

The red and blue songbird could not be apart.
They sang without care and with love in their heart.
They filled the spring air with harmony and peace
And somehow believed their love would not cease.

During the summer a robin flew by
And then the red songbird had caught his quick eye
The robin picked her flowers and her heart was won
So she flew off with him while leaving the one.

The songbird of blue now sang a sad tune
For she knew her lover would no longer swoon.
She couldn't be content as she was before
Songs lifted her spirits, but love made her soar.
Today, the blue songbird sings without end
In hopes that her lover will return once again.

Alexandra Estelle Hatch
Rome, GA

Unstable

I've tried to be strong...to hold on...to carry on
I've smiled when I felt like crying
I've overcome battles when I felt like dying
To be in my mind is a roller coaster ride
Keep face not to show what I'm feeling inside
So let's diagnose this with some self pity and stress
To hate everyone and feel like your life is a mess
But to hate is to show hatred and that I haven't done
I've always tried to shed light on those blocked from the sun
I've tried to be kind and to always stay true
And for some it's not enough and there's no more i can do
I've tried to speak out but only to find myself quiet
For I'm all alone with nothing but silence
Still my brain is a train running full steam
Filled with emotions not knowing what they mean
But my heart is not broken and it battles my brain
To a point where I feel like I'm going insane
Now it's taken a toll and my body feels weak
I wake up and wish I was still fast asleep
Dreaming sounds better than the reality of living
My mind says give up but my heart keeps on winning

Rebecca Lee Thompson
Myrtle Beach, SC

Where We Walk in Love

God isn't it lovely?
Oh so lovely
The way the grass
Touches your toes
Like sweet, wet pecks of passion.

Grazing your body,
Tracing its finger tips
Over your curves,
Whispering delicate
Songs of love

Smooth like icing
On chocolate cake.
Slowly
Swaying like tree tops
On a cool breeze.

God isn't it lovely?
I never thought
I'd love it this much.

Kaitlin Rose Spencer
Birdsboro, PA

When the Fog Lifts

When the fog lifts
Life was easy and simple before
Things were clear and easy to see
Then the fog came down and blurred the view
then I couldn't reach you
My love is just the same. That hasn't changed
I know that wrong was done. And I am the one to blame
But even though there is a haze we are still here
I will do my part to make this better
It will be such a gift if we are standing near each other
when the fog lifts.

Brian K. Landrum
Galena, AK

Magical Love

Opening my heart was hard.
But letting you in was even harder.
My walls were put up higher than the sky.
But my heart was open for love.
Love is the most amazing feeling in the world.
But my heart took time to find love for you. Trust is a issue.
Everyone destroys my heart.
So opening up for you was hard.
But when I finally did it was magical.
Your lips touching mine was like shooting stars.
Life is finally worthy of you.

Hannah Brooke Sathre
Nampa, ID

The Last Breath of a King

I fought my last battle in the trenches
I led my men to the heart of the beast
I struck the beast with every strength I had
The blade pierced the flesh of my enemies
My eniemes fell to their knees
As I stood over the beast with its head in my hands
But no matter how many deaths I bestowed upon
Nor how many times I saved my kingdom and the people
I could never account for my last breathe as king
The treachery of my own brother sleeping with the queen
To my queen poisoning my wine
Now I'm here on my last breathe asking for forgiveness
As I strike down my kingdom and the people I love
For tonight blood will spill one last time
The Fallen King

Herbert Lee Bynes
Fort Lauderdale, FL

My Mind Is a Prison

My mind is a prison,
And the sole inhabitants remain
My heart and soul,
Battering soft-feathered wings
Recklessly against the iron
Bars of the cage
That contains me.
My limbs are bound tightly
Rendered entirely useless—
Worthless,
My mind is a prison,
And I keep myself locked away
Behind the veneer of
A white picket fence,
A freshly-mowed lawn,
Trimmed hedges,
Gleaming windows,
A perfect 2.3 children life.
My mind is a prison,
And all the voices in it
Belong to a mental institution.

Unzila Mumtaz
Voorhees, NJ

Blue Balloon

On a sad day dear and fragile
I didn't know what to do
But I could not let myself unravel
So I stood and gave to you
Blue Balloon Blue Balloon
There was a quiet in the air
A melancholy tune
As it floated above you lying there
And read"Please get well soon"
Blue Balloon Blue Balloon
Filled with my hope and tears
It was weak beside your head
You and it are no longer near
It popped as your pulse rang dead
Blue Balloon Blue Balloon
On a sad day dear and fragile
I didn't know what to do
But I could not let myself unravel
There is nothing left of you
Blue Balloon

Justin Tyler Bloodworth
Macon, GA

Victory

In paradise you shall liey at rest
Rise to an occasion, in which
I will sob for you.
Invite your weary head into my bosom,
I shall hold your head up in pride.
Our tears will combine
and the sky will cry.
Home to the ruby red sands,
beds of forest mint
and leopards' fur,
you will return home,
my hand holding onto yours.
Your feet will stumble into the valleys of dignity.
My mind thinking of your pain and terror,
your body, a sacrifice for pleasure,
but no longer.
My soul weeps forgiveness for your heart,
your courage stands for us both.
My heart loves still all that harmed you,
the confusion of men at amazement.
Our cry will be heard.
Our victory shall rang.

Kiara Jones
Gainesville, FL

The Writer's Way

As the cadence of the typewriter begins to sway,
A cascade of words pours upon sheets of ghostly pallor.
And as a wave of lyrics surges upon my fingers,
The shards of my spirit are held together once again.
Within this sea of ebony ink,
Words that were once empty vials of meaning,
Come together to a rhythm no one shall disdain,
To hence compose a song of promise.
When these words are dealt with splendor,
One has the power to convey pure revelry or dismay.
To trap a reader in a tower of swirling intrigue,
Or to fly about lands so very far away.
With this power you shall unearth,
That with writing comes true valor.
A defiance greater than ammunition,
A revolver of prestige and prowess.
As my keyboard slows down its tempo,
I am left alone with a world of silence.
And as the tide of words returns ashore,
I return to my typewriter once more.

Sarah Flora Chocron
Wichita, KS

More Than Nature

I love you more than...
Trees love a summer's rain and
More than bees love honey

Darvonette Dyamond Abena Johnson
Richmond, VA

Save Me

Save me,
Please I have no where to be,
I just need help,
If you only knew how I felt.

I'm nobody now.
It's like music,
With no sound.
Only my life is where I'm bound.

You could of just helped,
You'll never know how I felt.

Brianna Michele Radcliff
Valdosta, GA

Pleasant

I hope this finds you pleasantly,
Without long regrets or sad bitterness.
I always thought you were the strong one
Out of all my useless friends.
Look at you now! How long it's been!
Heard you were some famous artist,
And you fell in love again.
I always thought you'd save your love for me.

I could never imagine selling myself.
That's something I saved for you.
Do you remember me?
Remember how it used to be?
When we'd share our music in the park,
We'd whisper lines of poetry in the dark,
I always loved you.

I don't even know who I'm writing this to.
If I met them now or later,
Or maybe it was another lifetime,
When I was a flower or a bird,
Or maybe in another world,
Another galaxy, far off, the unknown.
But you were always the one, the one I shared my stories to,
And no one really gets it quite like you

Erika R. Hamiter
Garfield Heights, OH

Bones

bones, brittle and thin
gasp for air as you swallow
you are now hollow

Caitlin R. Harris
Aurora, IN

Saltwater Songs: A Sonnet

Wake in the day by the beautiful light,
hear the roar of the ocean calling you.
Never can you wait for the starry night;
watch as the ocean turns a darker blue.
See the waves retreating, then coming back
as if an endless scene; walking in place.
No one can ever say that the ocean lacks
intensity. As if walking in place,
so in sync with time, crashing down with life.
The silver moon in the sky shines so bright.
I am caught up, it's hard to feel the strife
that comes in a package deal you can't fight.
So addicted to the saltwater songs
but we just have to stroll on right along.

Autumn Rose Pierce
Ashland, OH

Life

There's hurt feelings and pain
There's so much crying and rain
There's hitting and screaming
Tell me how to stop this feeling
Fear, anger, regret
This is something I can never forget
There's blood and bruises along her face
How I wish this image would erase
There's plea's for help
But no one listens
the sadness in my chest thickens
When she leaves only silence fills the house
Oh how I miss her in her ratty pink blouse
He drinks all his sorrows away
But his face still remains the same
Tears in his eyes and he knew
For the way he acted their love turned cruel
His regret can never fill this hole
Of all the anger in her soul
Even if she starts again
Her fear will always win

Alexis Sifuentes
El Paso, TX

Who Are You?

If I knew who I was
I would understand the plan
If I knew who I was
I'd be queen of the land
If I understood my thoughts
And placed them all in a row
Considered my conscious
And know what I know
Understand my actions
And work life as it flow
Make the right moves
Like I know where to go
Not thinking twice
Or second guessing myself
Strong in my choose
Taking life as it's dealt
If I knew who I was
I'd conquer my soul
Create my own destiny
And reach every goal.

Jelisa Jenkins
Humble, TX

Mind Vs. Humanity

I don't even know where to begin.
I can't fathom the words
to express my inner self.
To thy own self I can't be true!
I transformed myself to the purest form
in order to establish a higher connection
to another human to no avail.
The repercussions are both fatal
and irreversible,
even with every ounce of strength
from deep within the darkest corner of my soul,
It does not even begin to amount to anything
even remotely measurable,to this incurable
infection that is causing me to lose myself.
I am more detrimental to self now
than in any past recollection.
My appetite has tremendously increased due to the fact,
that commodity items are remotely the closest, cheapest,
and readily available serotonin booster on the market.
I am covered in self inflicted lacerations.
Moments of absolute torture!
Mind versus humanity.

Cristy Lynn Nelson
Miami, FL

Flowers, Flowers, Flowers

Scorching
Seven AM with its permissible air; though still scorching
Trudging from the G train towards an interview
I will take any job with AC
Which rules out:
Bryant Park
And Union Square Park
And those private West Side Parks
And the Brooklyn Botanical Gardens
And the New York Botanical Gardens
Almost there, when those flowers arranged in a quaint little change
Of scenery, in front of me
Hydrangeas and lilies and pansies and poppies
Struck me more than New York City's blasphemy;
Scorching
Those Cobble Hill flowers turned my trudge to a jig
And my mouth to a gape, passing drenched benches from sprinklers
That I gladly danced through, those flowers glistened and listened
To my woes and my throes before this interview
Flowers, flowers, flowers
Scorching hot flowers, colors louder than my nerves
I will be bold as their stance when I interview, when I dance
Wake me up, cool me down, sweep me gone, propel me on
To my interview, at Eight Thirty AM
Flowers, flowers, flowers

Kristen Hedberg
New York, NY

Subscriptions

I thank my hometown as a writer.
I do not know what fiction is or
what is the real thing.
Who else do I meet and who do
you write into your story?
But the fact is that I wrote
history instead, not just the main
character; I write all people.
I know my history when I watch
the page, which disappears
into the background.

Alyssa Matte
Stratford, CT

I am a senior at Susquehanna University, class of 2018. My majors are creative writing and studio art. I love writing pieces that give voices to those who don't have one and also writing about those topics that people choose to not speak about.

Am I Truly Wrong?

I love, I feel.
I struggle, I cry.
I dance, I hope.
I jump for joy.

So now tell me I am wrong,
for being a different color,
for being born of a different culture.
Tell me I am wrong
for liking a different approach,
for wanting to help and heal.
Tell me I am wrong
for being from a family of poverty, begging for a meal.

Why undermine those who are different?
Wouldn't life be a little bland if we were all the same?
Einstein was different. Abraham was different.
So why shouldn't we be different?
We all love,
feel,
struggle,
cry.
We dance, and hope.
We jump for joy.

Abby Malstrom
Wasilla, AK

The Scythe Weilder

You scared of the scythe wielder?
Always making people the yielder
With a dark ominous persona
Checking your soul's corona
Watching and waiting
Seeing you aging
He plans your demise
Comes to you, being a surprise
Yet, he doesn't kill you personally
He just"claims" people originally
He keeps an eye on everyone
And he can never be shunned
You could try to run and hide
Or be like some and commit suicide
But he comes none the less
Whether you're clean or a mess
But don't you worry, don't you worry
He'll lead you surly,
He'll lead you along to a better place
Or better hope you don't get the fire case

Sean Anthony Sawyer
Cabool, MO

Squirrel

I just went outside with my grandpa
we were sitting on the stoop
I saw a squirrel laying on the other side of the road
I went to go look at it
There was blood about a foot away from it
Judging by the lack of flies and decay
I think it died about a few minutes ago
its mouth was open
I was half frightened it would jump at me like"gotee"
There was a couple that walked past me looking at the dead squirrel
I waved and the man said"poor guy"
I went back to my grandpa and he said,"What'd you see?"
I said I saw a dead squirrel on the other side of the road
he asked,"Was it on the sidewalk or the road?"
I said it was on the road
then he said,"Oh, then it's roadkill. Oh yeah, I see it too"
I was surprised he could see that far
because his hearing isn't as good

Veronika Eva Kowalski
Brooklyn, NY

Naked Truth

for a woman to have such patience of 9 months
to produce life into this world
it's the most powerful form of love
it puts me on a pedestal.
if you have a fruit-shaped body part in between your legs
you're a blessing to mother nature
now, imagine the type of things men are thinking
in their heads, so small minded
blinded in their own ignorance.
see, mother nature is not lust
men of this generation are full of over-stimulation
of sexualizing the most beautiful creature close to God
yes, a woman's body, it's a work of art.
that also has a heart
from the start, it was created naked
to be accepted and appreciated, not hated but sacred
born in the human race to suffer the pain
that no man could ever endure.

Toby Ogbuaka
Richmond, TX

Vietnam

I am a lotus, once grown in the dirty, filthy mud
A flower that resonates with the sun and
the northern mountains filled with flood
I am a buffalo who is big, stubborn, dark-skinned, and slow
Who dwells in the green, breezy terraces, where the elegant rice grow
I am the calm river, home to the nine sons of the dragon
With fish sliding and chattering below
to the colorful boat folks above
I am a cunning cave whose beauty lies with pleasure
Underneath my heart lies its true treasure
I am a dragon who resides in the reflecting
emerald waters and towering rocks
Where the people live, they sing with their talks
I am the island who swims in the salty, sapphire sea
Whose coconuts jump and roll around in
the satisfying feeling of soft sand
I am the red and white scorching sand, always dancing with the wind
My friends fly bright kites, always laughing in the end
I am the bamboo tree who had seen the harsh times of war
Dreadful, it is, but determination and strength stands in my core
I am the imperial gate, overlooking the lives of my children
Small but sturdy, I protect them from all fierce villains
I am Vietnam who sits with my friends
and family in the southeast continent
My gifted people who dress fancy and
welcome you with smiles and content

Anh Le
San Jose, CA

Ode to You, Little Black Boy

As your mother and sister, I see your struggle.
I stand beside you and support that struggle.
You grow up hard with no one to love you.
It's the emptiness inside that makes you do what you do.
At the bottom of the food chain in this world we live,
Your face alone makes them shudder in fear.
So they mistreat you, and hold you down.
You get up fighting, trying to protect your crown.
You have so much potential, my sweet baby boy.
Don't let them hold you down and push you out the door.
Hold on to your gifts and continue to shine.
With intelligence, passion, and don't forget to be kind.
And oh my son, I'm here for you.
Only your mothers and sisters truly understand you.
We've been taught to hate ourselves and turn on one another.
But at the end of the day, you're still my son and brother.
You can't do this alone and you shouldn't have to.
Your family and GOD are here to support you.
We're ready when you are to take back your throne.
At the top of the food chain where mighty lions belong.

Bee Nance
Houston, TX

Our Soulmate

I'll be scared of losing my soulmate next time
I forgotten so many times that I love you
and it pleases you as my arms are wrapped around and in your being
while my eyes are open my enclosure to my own
interlaced perception of us which is non-existent
so of course yours closed in depersonalization
my back's being pricked and ledged of God's grace
I say I forget but I know in my heart I just push
the words down I love you gives
all my love pushed towards her enough of my belonging embedded
into the crocked brace evolved smile to have forgotten
I can never feel the same for myself more of myself I'd never heard
crying of and over the repetitions in my box
as my heart is pounding in my hands leading under
over my bladed amused flesh-colored paper
laughter filling my head as I'm just fawned over as
if her humor for me is love
threading a needle with the red over drawn my bottom lip
lapped of the juice of her womb bleeding my wrist
balanced of silence my hands up in fire
inside me shielded us burned by flowers molded over
the palm of her hand resting at an adjacent tilt of our own
inter salvaged fingers feeling like thorns inside her
and her dripping bed sheets
my necessity of her is humor
but never to her heart but never in her bed
but never am I or us not belonging

Janaija Mikala Leigh Ferguson
Benton Harbor, MI

Second Notion

Eye to eye,
quick look away.
Scorned delicate flesh,
iron brandings of heat.

Shuffled person to person,
yet same unprobed fascade.
Confused nonchalant emotions,
heart break on repeat.

Idolized the essence of love,
yet fears vulnerability.
Subconscious theory—
"No exposure, hence no risk."

Contemporary gallantry,
dinner's entitlement to "dessert."
Cannot commit too prematurely,
forgive me for I am not too brisk.

Latoya Riddick
Daytona Beach, FL

People, Places, and Things

People live and they die
People can't hold us though they try
Places are built and torn down
Places hold memories but not a crown
Things are pretty and can be taken
Things try to control you, but they're very mistaken
People aren't going to keep me from my blessing
Places aren't going to remind me of my past stressing
Things aren't going to ruin my appointing
God is going to lead me to my anointing

Dyesha Donae Moore
Benton Harbor, MI

Tuesday Shine

She winks as if to tell a story,
The brightest grin I've ever seen,
The source of all my pain and glory;
Shines her rays upon my skin.
Her simple, yet, potent fare,
Gives the world a gift of rainbow,
To which I lend my eager eyes,
As I stand directly below.
As she prepares to lay to rest,
She promises another day.
I see her off into the sunset,
And go on my merry way.

Anna Pi
Valley Village, CA

Letters to My Tenants

Dear happiness
The next time you arrive please stop having house parties;
the neighbors don't like it.
I'm not sure if anybody wants your "friends" to uh—
clog up the halls?
Dear sadness
You and your cousins depression, regret and guilt need to
notify me of when you're crashing happiness' party because
regret keeps to the walls but everyone's uncomfortable
guilt likes to make everything about him
and depression ALWAYS
a l w a y s
brings uninvited guests
Dear anxiety
I don't understand why you keep tagging along with depression;
nobody wants you there, you're just like Becky with her bad
Waldorf salad that literally
nobody
will eat please just get out nobody wants you
I don't want you
I don't want me
Dear brain
Every time more houseguests push their way in,
you and yours push me out.
Thanks,
The Management

Jessica Smith-James
Corvallis, OR

Feel

I can still feel the warmth inside when I knew I loved you.
I can feel my hands twirling through
the locks of Heaven that lay on your head.
I can still feel your chiseled face after a haircut
as you rub your face across mine.
The deep talks, relaxation sensation that provided us with
a sense of safe will never leave me.
When you hurt, I feel it.
When you're happy, I feel it.
When you're mad, I feel it.
It's a feeling that can't be explained or deranged
into something that doesn't make sense
because all the sense lies within.
We, together, make sense.
You feel for me as I feel for you.
We feel for each other.

Ariana Janay Yvonne Stevens
Los Angeles, CA

Highs and Lows

I've spent countless
Hours at the beach
Watching the tide
Come and go
And I often wonder
What kind of love
Makes the ocean
Move to every
Whim of the moon
Without ever asking
For anything in return
But then again
I'm not sure I know
What love is myself

Ibrahim A. Mustapha
Monroe, LA

Tangerine

I am not
A tangerine
To pick open and consume
My insides
Are supple
Not created for you.
Allow my body to pass
With time
Gently
As a withering stone

Delilah Miske
Philadelphia, PA

Shattered

I breathe in
Then scream out
Nothing's wrong, don't know what it's about
Been lying here
For days now
I try to think
But can't now
I'm shattered
What you did to me
Took me to cloud nine
Then dropped me
And what for?
But to catch her
Falling for you
You dropped me
I loved you
But you loved her
You shattered me
Just like glass
Completely forgetting
About our past
But now all I do is laugh
Because I know
She doesn't love you back
She only loved him
Who dropped her

Nirvana Rachelle Cupp
Batesville, AR

Answered Prayers

My heart's been broken a time or two...
Was it not made for a love that's true?
While the question frequently crosses my mind, it simply cannot be...
For my heart is the biggest part of me.
I live and I laugh and I always love...
Most importantly, I pray to the Man above!
I prayed to God for the love of my life...
Someone who would love me enough to one day make me his wife.
The prayers went unanswered but I kept praying anyway...
Then, I met you that one summer day!
I was beat down, broken and had lost my joy...
I walked away, looked to God and asked, is this him or another decoy?
As time progressed, things became clear...
The man I had prayed for was standing right here.
There's a connection between us I cannot deny...
But I sit here silently as I fear your reply.
Could you feel the same...could I be what you need?
Can we join hands in this thing called life and succeed?
Answers to these questions I do not know...
But my love for you continues to grow.
I don't know what the future holds...
Or exactly how our story unfolds.
I know what I want...it's truer than true.
I want to take this journey through life with you!

Tanya D. Childress
Floresville, TX

Feat

At forty-five my whole life changed,
My future came faster than I had dreamed.
What laid beneath my blinded eyes,
Cancer was found which no one denies.
At first I was in deep despair,
I thought for sure my end was near.
I cried and thought what must I do,
For I knew not what I believed was true.
Although these thoughts did not last long,
If I thought of death it would be wrong.
I knew I was a constant fighter,
And I knew that I must be a survivor.
So I set my path before my feet,
And walked that path towards the feat.
I rose above the challenging despair,
And knew my life would end up fair.
I believe with positive thought,
I cured myself with what I fought.
Don't get me wrong I had help medically,
The people, the surgery, radiation totally.
I thank them all for saving my life,
They worked so hard and were concise.
I thank myself for staying strong,
Because of this world I still belong.

Cori Eschenbach
Los Angeles, CA

Daddy's Little Girl

I was little, I was naive
I was too small when you made me believe
I was young so you took your time
To break down my spirit and take away the shine
With every year we began to fear
The time with you was drawing near
You shattered my spirit and killed my youth
You made me believe your sermons were truth
The devil would remain if I told a lie
And to hell I would go when I die
At times you let her chase us away
So we wouldn't be a bother and wouldn't stay
She tricked us with chemicals, evil, and death
She made us believe we were worthless
and needed to take our last breath
You let her chase me from door to door
And she always caught me because my weight was poor
You let your friend almost break my arm
And wouldn't believe me that he meant me harm
You were never there to bring us joy
We were never the same girl and boy
Religion was the punishment, it was your greatest tool
You locked us away because you were so cruel
I loved you too much so I would believe
That you would protect me and never leave

Alexandria Fons
Oklahoma City, OK

The Scorpio

The dreamer who some might call,
he seeks only one who can make his heart fall.
One woman whose beauty is hard to find,
but loves her more because of her heart and mind.
He is courageous and will defend her, too,
protect her heart from me and you.
Because she is the only one who shows him light,
even on the darker days when it's as dark as night.
But let it be known if you misguide his soul,
his time is the only thing you have wasted and stole.
His trust for you will be lost and you will be left with awe,
even if you are perfect and have no flaw.
But keep his love and hold it tight, he will forever be yours.
He will be your
Mr. Right

Richard Summers
Dickinson, TX

I Thought I Had a Job

I thought I had a job.
He paid me to do awful things to him
And I was only thirteen.
Alone in the house with an older man.
A family friend I thought I could trust.
His money was so available.

He molested me
And told me it was my work.
I thought it was my fault.
I could not tell my mother for years.
Back then I thought I had a job.
I carry the burden still.

Kerri Snow
Liberty, NY

Refracted Dreams

I dived into your eyes
wanting to be baptized.
I could not see past lies;
I could not see past seven feet marker signs.
Refraction is the mistress giving birth to stillborn dreams.
Now, I close my eyes and bow my broken neck
because I could not see from on high
that water was ten miles wide
but only two inches deep.

Byung In Yoo
Anaheim, CA

Death I Fear

Wake up in a drench of sweet.
Tremble from the dreams of defeat.
Drown into the deepest sea. This is me.
Fear is real.
Fear is all I feel. Death I fear.
Fall deep into a dream. I wake with a loud scream.
Tumble from a building high, but wake before I know if I die.
Fear is intense.
Fear is never dense. Death I fear.
The building rocked, and broke loose, it tumbled over and over.
My family and I called to each other, the voices.
Then I could hear no others.
I woke again my dream felt as though it was so real.
My heart beat so fast, I could not breath.
I walked around looking in on my children, beautifully sleeping.
My fear of death overwhelmed my sleep.
It is deep and real. Death I fear.
Looking in as his body hung lifeless.
Tears streamed from the faces of loved ones in disbelief.
Cut him down to the ground.
Death is unknown.
Death is sudden. Death I fear.

Melinda Kay Chairez
West Lafayette, IN

All Her Life

All her life
She was as lonely as a widow
No true, genuine friends
She never spoke
Because if she were to
Everyone would yell their burning, heart-wrenching words at her
All her life
She was as lonely as an elderly lady in a nursing home
While everyone talked to their friends down the narrow school halls
She clung to her tear-filled books
Words were her only friends
She lived for their knowledge.
All her life
She was as lonely as Rose after her Jack died
When she would get home, she would cry her broken heart out
Her room was empty, quiet, and pitch-black
To cover her appearance that nobody liked
To hide her tears that would continue falling forever

Alyssa Rae Mercedes Pham
Cantonment, FL

Growth

Trees and grass go away so fast,
They take so long to grow,
We must take time and effort,
We must let Mother Nature know,
We will stand together,
To keep the world clean,
We will raise money and start a green team,
We rescue dying animals,
From other peoples polution,
We will work together to find a solution.
We need determination,
We need to keep hope,
So we will work together,
To ensure plant growth.
I hear birds chirping,
I hear trees in the wind,
Here is where our destiny begins.

Dee Anna Sanders
Sopchoppy, FL

My Mother's Kindness

Every night I was alone
I hear crying in the distance
My crying
I cry every night and think about what I did
Did I hurt my family?
Do I have a purpose in life?
Why am I still here?
A little part of me dies when I see my mother crying
I tried suicide to end all this hardship
But I couldn't bring myself to do it
I think, will I be able to remember the smiling faces of my family?
Will I remember my mother?
Will my mother be sad?
One day my mother found me trying to suicide
Before I knew it I started to cry
My mother cried and hugged me
She was sad that I had done this
She said, "Don't ever do anything like this again
You are just being selfish"
I understood what my mother had felt
I'll love her until I rest

Kao Nou Thao
Appleton, WI

Social Media

You check your phone again,
Sifting,
Searching,
Hunting,
Looking,
For affirmation from a screen,
Posting for the pleasure of acceptance,
Staring wishfully at others posts,
Wishing,
Wanting,
Hoping,
You were like them,
They always seem to have the perfect,
House,
Hair,
Friends,
Clothes,
So you post,
Just to start the cycle again,
Waiting,
Watching,
Hoping,
That you get more followers than them,
Fully submerged in that world,
But unaware that it has consumed you.

Courtney Ann Bender
Lincoln, NE

Ode to Bearded Men

When I lay my head on my pillow
I can feel my heart beat between my sheets
I lie here under the inflictions of your uncertainty
The difference of your words
The absence of your somber
Of your sobriety
Of your eagerness to please
And maybe we will be in love someday
When you are no longer Peter Pan with facial hair
Because I need a man, not a boy
I know that I am the top of your list
But I'm not your forever drinking partner
I am your convenient
Your naked goddess
Your bad girl, eager for your palms pressed against my throat
Waiting for the time you push and hold
Too long, too hard
I am the girl at the end of the day
"You can come over, if you want"
He would say
While I write him poems and listen to
Playlists I made him on Spotify
This is a poem to the boy I thought man
An ode to the could have beens

Naomi Retter
Riverview, FL

The Last Moment

I lay here empty,
numb to all pain and sorrow.
A tear rolls down my cheek,
it is not warm like any other but is
calming by how frigid it feels.
I breath in deep,
feeling as if a weight has been lifted.
I look around,
my surroundings are becoming dark.
I am not afraid,
I am relieved and at peace.
I close my eyes tightly,
I see only the memories that kept my
heart beating.
Now I feel nothing,
no pain, no sadness, no anger.

Chelsie Poffenberger
Alliance, OH

An Expected, Unexpected Surprise

I sense it, before I see it
the sweet droplets of water
falling from the sky.
As they hit the ground
in a uniform pitter-patter
penetrating the earth,
and soaking beneath its surface.
The smell of the moist,
New Mexican dirt
floods my nose with its
fresh, muddy scent.
This is an unexpected surprise
like it normally is,
the rain.

Lanie Perez
Rio Rancho, NM

1000 Likes

You and I, side by side
Your world, my world—all aligned.
Yet so distant, countless miles,
Bring me back my stolen smiles.

You didn't know something was missing?
Didn't understand we weren't kissing?
Perhaps I am a foolish man
Trying to save just what I can.

Our love, so great, above it all
It makes me bleed, it makes me fall.
A force that strikes
With sharpest spikes,
Can you give this a 1000 likes?

Oksana Goodin
West Chester, OH

The Stasis of Downward Emotions

Is it so bad
that I cannot remember
a single happier time?
When skies were bluer
and life ran smoother.
But all I have known
is tragedy after tragedy
catastrophes one after another
crowded and twisted and stacked.
Why is it that everything must be
so fragile and delicate
that silence is painful
while noise simply is?
And everything I ever wanted
is so immensely
out of my reach.

In asking all of these questions
I thought I would find
a reason?
That life went so wrong . . .
Maybe life didn't go wrong
I just have a skewed version of right
In this,
The stasis of downward emotions.

Alanna Grace Camargo
Saratoga Springs, UT

Evergreen

How lucky am I, to walk through these deep dark woods?
From gloom to doom to tomb.
Let me rest where the still fawn rests.
Where the worst of worsts is equal to the best of bests.

Ashes and dust,
the underground mine,
to steel and restless rust.

How lucky am I, this hemlock dream?
Evergreen.

Peter Valley
Houston, TX

The Perfect Storm

She stands, a glow on her face
Her mouth a crescent smile
Glitter in her eyes as she laughs
Her personality igniting a fire in others
She's the center of attention
The life of every party
She puts the room at ease with her presence
Not a care in the world
Outgoing. Infectious. Happy
Underneath the perfect exterior
Lies the aftermath of a tornado
A lonely town that cannot be put back together
Torn and tattered
Disheveled
Broken and battered
One by one they get pulled away
She is alone.
Her eyes spill tears of pain and sorrow and loneliness
She cowers to the ground and screams
but only the silence of her pain is heard
She begs for someone to notice her
For someone to love her
But all she sees is darkness
So she moves about
In the only way she knows how
As the loneliest, happiest girl in the world
Knowing inside that nobody knows her pain

Whitney Rubin
Chesterfield, MO

Go for the Prize

Growing up being called ugly
It left a scare on my soul
And as I got older
That irrelevant phrase, took its toll
The low self esteem
Gave off this crazy scent
So every relationship I encountered
Ended in wasted time spent
I use to hate to look at myself
In the reflector called the mirror
Back then most days a towel covered it
Now, uncovered, I look and smile every now and then
I need to get over this fear
Self-love should be authorized;
Deep down I know the result
Happiness will be the prize

Shannah Hazel Beckett
Hackensack, NJ

America's No Longer Great

America, what happened? You used to be so great.
But, now, you're a society of bullying and hate.
From talk show hosts, comedians, reporters "on the scene,"
it seems that everything you do—and listen to—is mean!
Celebrities flaunt excess; explicit, vulgar tones.
Your leaders all resort to hard profanity on phones.
The Facebook posts are bawdy, show shoddy disrespect;
and this comes from America, one nation we'd expect
to be a bit more civil and be much more urbane.
Instead, we see a country that's led by the insane!
Your president just tweeted, "The world is watching!" —Yes!
And I'm quite sure they're laughing (unless I miss my guess).
America, what happened? For all the world you've been
a beacon. What's it going to take to make you great—again?

Ron Oetting
New Haven, IN

Since August 2015 it's been a distrubing political season. Vicious accusations, hellish hyperbole, and not much substance have dominated what appears to be a weakened, decaying political process. Bath then I started writing my "Political Poetry By RKO" and I've continued composing a poem a day ever since. I hope you enjoy my tongue-in-cheek utterances as much as I've enjoyed writing them. And I hope you'll share them with your friends and neighbors. Who knows what kind of deliberations it might incite over an ice cold beer, a smooth red wine, or a raucous rum and cola? Cheers!

We Can Make a Change

There is a world of people,
Waiting to explore.
There is a world of people,
Always wanting more.
But how can we,
Escape the world around us.
But how can we,
Find a world that's lost.
Can you find it in your heart and soul,
To persevere.
Can you find it in your heart and soul,
To change the world you hold dear.
There is a world of people,
Waiting to explore.
There is a world of people,
Always wanting more.
We can do it,
We can make a change.
We can do it,
We can do it on a wide range.

Payton Avila
Oakdale, CA

Worth of a Woman

A Woman is the fruit of Life,
A Woman is the key to a Man door.
Exactly what you need to complete your emptiness.
A Woman worth is a strong value,
Sometimes men often jeopardize a woman worth
For something of know value.
A Woman can be the finish before you cross the line.
The thing you need the key, Worth of a woman.

Dwight Drummond
North Lauderdale, FL

Eighteen

I've been thrown into a fight, but told not to hit back.
I've been given dozens of millions of dollars to track.
I've jumped from very high things that worked perfectly good.
I've left many nice girls, I doubt they understood.
I've seen people broken and known many kinds of pain.
And I've lied on their surveys, so they'd have proof I was sane.
I've known young people that died, I've heard cries and moans.
I've been worked like a serf but drawn far far from home.
I have been paid in dollars I could not live to spend,
and if I was eighteen, I'd do it again.

John Dominic Gordon
Tampa, FL

Thoughtful Love

I think of you when I wake in the morning,
and when I close my eyes at night.
I think of you when the rain falls outside
and when the sun is shining bright.

I think of you when I'm stuck in traffic,
and when I'm home watching my show.
I think of you when I'm on a plane ready to fly,
and when I'm walking somewhere real slow.

Love doesn't keep time or limit itself
to a certain race or breed.
Love has no boundaries or restrictions.
It's everywhere there is a need.

I think of you when my heart is full,
and when my glass is half empty.
I think of you when no one is watching,
and when the grass on the other side is tempting.

I think of you without even trying,
and in crazy amounts when I do.
I think of you all the time every day,
and when I want to say I love you.

Love doesn't keep time or limit itself
to a certain race or breed.
Love has no boundaries or restrictions.
It's everywhere there is a need.

Rachel Hawks
Climax, NC

Unruly Soul

My soul feels like it has been ripped out of my body,
My mind slipped away.
My heart is numb and has locked itself away.
My soul is tired,
Tired of being hurt,
Tired of all the jokes against me,
Tired of trying to explain one self to others.
For others who don't want to understand,
Why i have been an unruly soul.
My unruly soul feels safe where it is.
It can feel as numb as it can be.
It won't bother me ,
I want to stay locked away because,
I can't hurt no one.
My unruly soul can rest until it feels,
it's no longer going to be hurt again.
But for my unruly soul that day will come
soon enough,
As the years go by it will finally
lay to rest.
Rest in peace you unruly soul.

Donna Tymec
Kankakee, IL

Resurfacing

Have you ever felt the sensation of drowning?
Your heart pounds, pulse quickens, mind races.
You think: this is it. This is my demise.
You long for air as your lungs plead for oxygen,
So close, yet so far.
You don't know which way is up and which is down.
All you can think of is that delicious gasp of air that awaits you.
But what if you never came back up?
What if you stayed down so long that you became the water itself?
You long to swim to safety, but no matter how hard you try,
You can't get out of the water.
You're drowning.
You kick and fight until you can no longer bear the agony.
You gasp in the water, succumbing to your fate.
But it isn't death that awaits.
It's relief.
Soft, sweet, relief.
The pain is gone because you're no longer fighting.
Your fate is sealed.
Your bed is made.
But you're no longer in agony.

Donise Michelle Sheppard
Delbarton, WV

Rising Sun

You think I'm an angel from the sky
But I'm a demon in disguise
I'm someone you wouldn't recognize
So close your eyes
Don't look at me,
I'm struggling to break free
From the binds, tying me down, to the ground
I want to fly, instead I run
Chasing the fleeing sun
Fighting to stay awake
So I won't remember my past mistakes
There is only so much I can take
Before I finally break
You can't kiss the hurt away
My scars aren't skin deep
I don't want to fall asleep
Please keep me awake
So the nightmares won't come
Before the rising sun

Christina Marie Combs
Leonardtown, MD

With Genuine Regret

My dearest love, oh how I have missed you
every second of each minute
every minute of each hour
As I sit here bewildered and deeply saddened, reminiscing
our high school years are gone, the college days so far away
but your voice still so clear
your touch so warm
awake, I think of you
asleep, I dream of us
my presence is unwanted, I know
My name, you wish to forget
I am ashamed for the way I put down
I am sadden for making you feel small
the fire in my soul still burns for you
our souls were meant to be, why can't you see
forgive me, I am on my knees
let us bury the hatchet, please
with genuine regret, I am sorry
for the pain I caused us both, I am guilty
I never stopped loving you, the possibility of it, is slim
my walls were up, my heart was closed
my emotions were chained with distrust
our separate ways, we went
when the stars align, find your way back to me, I pray
for whatever it takes, I'll do.

Tanya Kamwanya
Woodbridge, VA

Stressed Out

I'm always stressed
College is only a few years away
And you might have guessed,
I am unprepared for that day
So many decisions to make
So little time,
The only thing worse is this headache
I have to choose and quickly too
But I haven't a clue
What I'll choose as my major
And I thought being a teenager,
Was the hardest part of life
But my life has only begun.

William Hunter Tatum
Oxford, MS

My Flies and Me

The real issue for writing is not ideas.
Ideas are easy,
They fly in and around.
They land when an emotion or memory or experience calls them out.
The problem is they are fleeting fast frightful delightful flies,
Flying through a moment,
Through your head,
Through your eyes,
They mock you with the imprint they leave behind,
And what's worse is they are never just one flying ahead or around.
No! All the foes flood in at once!
Flinging themselves at you,
Flooding your system,
Till drowning,
Till overlong you frightful scream out!
And then they all disappear, but a few.
And those are never the full picture,
They never fit the film that flowed in your head
Just moments ago music,
Now a jaunted haunted jagged flat piece of shit.
They were once a symphony if I could just make them fit.
Trap all my ideas like flies.
And sort them at night.
Oh, what a writer I would be!
I would finally be free,
My flies and me.

Brynna Bridges
Summerville, GA

Unable to Go Back

Unable to go back.
Fearful of going forward.
Stuck here, now.

Retaliation like a boomerang
Overcome by regret.
Giving into sorrow.
I'm tired.
Wanting to sleep.
Wanting to foget.
At the mercy of forgiveness, knowing they will not forget.

Words spoken in anger, the lack of love and respect.
Rejection familiar.
My life's biggest regret.
Unable to go back.

Christine Murphy-Flynn
Newport, MI

Broken

The crack in my heart was small and untouched.
When you came along and planted your seed,
I thought it filled the gap.
Your roots dug deep and your flower bloomed,
making me feel exotic and desired.
But when the season ended,
your flower wilted,
and I was left more broken than when you found me.

Paige Wilde
Sandy, UT

The Baby I Miss

For it to be,
but not exist
My sisterhood to see
That all but one consists
Only two were well
Except the early demise
Of the one I could never meet,
But saw with my own eyes
With her warm blanket on lifeless feet
For her cold forehead lied a kiss
The first and last of the baby I miss

Mariel Gonzalez
Alburtis, PA

American Military

It's time for Americans to take a stand,
by honoring those who defend our land.
They have gone places no one wanted to be,
defending this country by land, air and sea.
We Americans are known as the brave and the free,
but has anyone wondered how this came to be.
Please take a minute and listen to me and
I'll show you how American spells military.

The first A is for air force,
then M for marines,
E is for enlisted women and men,
R is for reserves,
I stands for infantry,
C is for coast guard,
the second A stands for army
and last but not least N stands for navy and national guard.
This is my greatest hope you will see,
this country would be nothing without our military!
I would just like to take this time to show all branches of military
whether you are current, a veteran, or God's taken you home,
how much I respect and appreciate each and every one of you
and the sacrifices you've made defending this country and
making me proud to say I am an American!
May God bless and keep you safe from all harm
until you are back safely home
with your families or in the Lord's arms. Amen and Thank you!

Kristi Darlene Stillion
Cambridge, OH

Night Rides

I call down to the people below
"Come with me," Icarus to the moonlight
My arms outstretched
a human glider, fluid air,
faster,
freer than thought.
My twin brothers scream, waking my bliss
from sleep to
reality.
"Daddy's gettin' Mom again."
Groggy, I hear china shatter,
chairs overturned.
My mother's cry.
QT says dreams are my escape valve
to sanity. He should know.
He left his legs in Viet Nam.
Oh QT,
the cold ledge from my third story window
seems too narrow for my size seven feet.
No matter,
I realize I don't need
sleep
to fly.

Regina Marie Anagnostis
Whiting, NJ

Too Late

Looking around for the familiar face, the face of home
Searching beyond the corners and closed doors
Frantic to see the smile that always eased the pain
To feel the comfort that I wasn't alone
Looking down hallways running to reach the end,
But it continues on
Calling out but no response
The hallway turns to grass
Granite marking the aisles, so many aisles surround me
Running and running the markers lead to one
Hard to read at first then the writing becomes clear
Panic jumps the dreamer and awakens from the nightmare
Only it is not a nightmare,
Reality sets in and the same feelings emerge again
There will not be any comfort given, only that in memory
No stories to share in person, no advice to be received
No chance to say I'm sorry

Wendy L. Averill
Poland, ME

The Fork in the Dust

the outline of the future,
for fates hand to weave,
the fork in the dust
would mark the end
of the reprieve.
diverged,
or
converged,
true love was conceived
she would always burn for love,
his tears may yet unfreeze..
if only every scar believed.
when and if they are
released anew
as one, or as two
upon a wild and undamned flow
on currents of tears shedded blue
headed to the deepest, stillest pool,
as glassy as a mirror but
unbreakably true.
they were streaming all along
on the never ending.

Shannon Alyssa Santucci
Page, AZ

Society

You marveled at my bravery
And told me that I was strong,
So I conquered your fears laughing
To prove you weren't wrong.
But as I chased your demons over the hill
To show you there are no monsters here,
I came to realize that you and I
Have very different ideas of fear.

You fear failing in the public gaze,
 I fear making them proud.
You fear spiders, steep mortgages, marrying too late,
I fear naming my horrors aloud.
You fear others and I fear myself.

And they say that real courage
Isn't the lack of fear but facing it instead,
Yet as I finally look in the mirror
All I'm faced with is dread.
Because somehow the very fear
I've been running from has come true;
You see, what I was scared of all along
Was simply becoming you.

Sawyer Emily Scott
Denton, MD

The Soliloquy of My Song

My song prevails as my sole medicine,
Ethereal sounds swung in a lilted draft
Tearing deeply into my skeleton,
Due to be determined unsurpassed.
So awfully loud my spirit rises
With religious, profound exhales of life,
Grieving emotional sacrifices
Chiseled by my driven, unconscious knife.
Forget-me-nots will blossom my winters;
Apprehensions will shadow my summers;
Sanguine impressions will quell my center
For lullabies succeeding my slumber.
One eloquent, sovereign voice stands strong;
She spars for recognition of her song.

Anna Teresa Ames
Tampa, FL

There Is a God

The trees are drifting and the wind is filling up the sky.
The mountains is covering up part of the sun.
Everything plays its roles.
Everything that happens is in its place.
You wonder who could make the sky blue and the clouds white?
God, he created all of this.
He is the reason why gravity is not so high on Earth.
Through dirt and nature,
Humans is what he birthed.
He breathed his life into us.
He gave us a ground to walk on,
He gave us streams of water to drink on.
What atom or cell could ever do that?
You should all know these things are all miracles.
So everytime you see a leaf falling,
or rain coming out of the clouds,
Just think of God because there is one.

Antwanette Howard
Dallas, TX

Stones

Stones—ancient,crude, and forlorn—
defied the soybeans and corn
which in turn assailed
their corner of the field.

Round-up could not control
them like weedy greenery.
So one night an evil troll
piled them around a tree.

The eternal spirits did not moan
for faded reminders of the unknown.
Forgotten now their living past
along with markers hoped to last.

Mourn them not their nameless existence.
Rather marvel at the corn's persistence.
Their fate surely we will share,
and only the soybeans will really care.

Joseph Charles McGuire
Boston, KY

You Broke Me

Your eyes sink into my soul,
the longer you stare,
the deeper you go.
I want to tell you no,
but my brain won't stop saying go.
Before I know it you're there;
I look down and I'm missing my underwear.
I don't think I feel fear,
but I know I absolutely don't want to be here.
You keep going,
and now it hurts.
You pay no mind to what I want;
it hurts now I'm begging you please stop.
I push but I have no strength.
I cry but no one's there to hear my pain.
Is this all I am?
A body to be used for male contentment?

For you that night was fun.
For you that night was games.
But for me that's when I broke,
and now I can't feel anything but pain.

Kali Ella Baker
Santa Rosa, CA

Radio Flyer

From radio flyer to American liar
The boomers just move on.
Listen to no one . . . grab for it all . . .
Justify the con.
Older not wiser . . . addicted to greed.
Care not who suffers...
Fill dysfunctional need.
Osama was evil . . .
or was he sent
By an angry God
Who wanted to vent?
There are no accidents
the message is "get it"!
But they can't leave their toys
So on they just let it!

Nancy G. Larson
Menomonie, WI

The Empty Boat

Free oneself from clinging to the river's edge,
Letting go with faith into the flow,
Unresisting, no aversion to where one may go.

Traveling as a passenger with no destination,
One with the water the vessel is free of care,
No name, no home, no attachments to bear.

Simple is oneself, within and without,
By all appearances one may seem a fool,
No desire to shout or fear of ridicule.

Without judgment, without reputation, no story,
Passenger becomes pilot at one with the sea,
Way of the enlightened, the boat is empty.

Randall Douglas Scott
Graham, NC

Lies

Misery
Destruction
Despair
Unhappiness
Death
No one is perfect
But you must strive to be perfect
So when you lie part of you dies
Don't die stay alive
Live long
Live life to the fullest!
To the highest!
To the happiest!
Don't mope in your misery
Don't die inside
Bring light to the world and yourself!
Good night!

Cordelia Rose Padovan
Ballston Spa, NY

Through a Child's Eyes

Through a child's eyes
Color is like a veil
Misleading when interpreted and sincere when ignored
The hue of man is no more eminent than a surface
Which bears nil resemblance to the interior
Yet endows uniqueness in the likeness of a rainbow.
Through a child's mind
Hope is like a breeze
Tinged with the fresh fragrance of sweet sun
And worry, a gale before a tempest
Both opaque in form yet distinct in aura
While hope is a blessing and worry, a curse.
Through a child's ears
War is like a storm
A cacophony of the lightning and thunder of enmity
In which peace is the rain, the purifying tears of nature
She cleanses the agony of the skirmishes of the heart
And seeps with silence into the serenity of the soul.
Through a child's heart
Love is like a blossom
Flourishing in spring's garden among the stifling weeds of hate
All gardens yield both crops
Though the one which acquires the greater nourishment
Reproduces and determines the outcome of the hour of harvest.
Only a child is not yet tainted by the inevitable biases of the world
Through a child's eyes, he is the future.

Fiona Aileen Sauve'
Gilbert, AZ

Shoulders

It curves gracefully
just like the neck,
yet it denotes purity,
an angelic effect,
flows like streams,
velvety eminence,
like a cry to be touched,
they bear their innocence.

Natasha Dillon Brieker
Mehoopany, PA

From the Heart

I love it when I think of you.
I love the way we touch.
I love the way your eyes shine so blue.
Oh how I love you so much.
Your heart so pure and innocent, your arms so strong yet tender.
Your voice so warm and soothing, it's my heart I surrender.
I love the way you're compassionate and kind.
You were trustworthy from the start.
Forever and always, I love you with all my heart.

Emily Grace Keene
McCalla, AL

Views of the World

Too many girls up in this world
that are so insecure
I'll try to tell you differently
but lately i'm not sure
Looked in the mirror
and I saw what other people see
I looked inside
and I felt what I could truly be
I used to be the girl
who felt the need to be at home
stayed in my room
and I tried my best to be alone
But life had looked at me
and said that I could do some more
Closed up my insecurities
And just opened a door
So now i'll tell you differently
we are amazing girls
And I can tell just by your smile
that we can change the world

Lexis Ca'netta Cobb
Louisville, MS

Don't Let Go

Remember that the sun won't always shine
when everything is fine.
And rain never falls
when the feeling calls.

It's funny how the moon
isn't always round,
but it never makes a sound
when it calls a hound.

But one thing is for sure—
the sound of the ocean
is always there to allure.
The waves are always in motion,
forever coming back to shore
and coming back to you.

That's devotion.

Sara Roderick
New York, NY

The Modern Day

We grew up without words like terrorists
And ISIS and Al-Queda and no-fly lists
Were raised to worship and follow God
Not living in fear of Jihad
United we stand, so you attack us all
Even just one, together we'll fall
But all as one, we shall rise
And stop believing your terrorist lies
When going to concerts and shows was the norm
A suicide bombers perfect storm
Planes and trains and trucks and cars
They're pushing our limits, when is too far?
Mosques and churches and clubs and schools
What is one supposed to do?
The flowers and memorials and ribbons and wreaths
And all the souls that lie beneath
We, too, shall strike, don't you fret
And disrupt your networkss, you can bet
For you must pay for all this death
The ultimate price, your final breath
The evil you've caused and all who have died
Your day is near, nowhere to hide
This is for all of the ones that we miss
'Cause we grew up without words like terrorist

Robert Vesper
Waupun, WI

I Don't Understand

I just cannot understand
Why doesn't anybody take a stand?
We sit there and watch it
Not knowing she's just a misfit
Nobody really knows
Why it's the decision she chose
But she is all alone
Has no place to call home
She puts the razor to her wrist and slits away
When she was gone nobody had any words to say
But you knew all along
You tried telling her she was strong
You didn't get her any support
You let her disappear through the port

Bennayah Lejae Collier
Raleigh, NC

It's Just Me Being Me

It's just me being me
It's relaxing time and I'm online
I like the taste of sweet champagne
It takes away my bitter pain
And I don't enjoy to wake up
 I tend to rub off my make-up, and sometimes I'm up at ten
still directing my pen
It's just me being me
I'm also an am/pm kinda girl
Waking up early in this
sleepy world
Time to let my day start before the darkness part
and let the sunlight shines
in the depths of my heart
until it sparkle and have an aura of purple, until my written words
become verbal
It's just me being me

Vanessa S. Khorn
Sacramento, CA

The Sun Will Shine Again

The sun will shine another day
I will get through the rain,
And on the other side I'll see,
I have much more to gain.
With head held high, praise be to God,
For showing me somehow,
That even when I'm at the lowest,
I can stop and thank him for now.
We never know what is ahead,
That's how it's supposed to be,
And we will look back on this trial,
It's then that we will see.
In the moment, you cannot see,
It's a blessing in disguise,
What you pray for today, may not be your tomorrow,
And you'll see with unclouded eyes.
Trust in him, pave your way, keep head up, you are free,
To do what your heart, wants for you, be whatever you want to be.

Maureen Theresa Hart
Dartmouth, MA

A Break in the Waves

Still-frame scenery, subtle skies
A snap and the waves begin to crash
A mind once held together by the ropes of sanity
Is now an unleashed plethora of white doves, innocent
And bearing your memories
As the memories fly, disappearing from sight, you forget
The skies transform, the water opaque
And flooding the mind
The coordinates you followed are gone
And you can no longer see the land
That was once your point of security
Frightening and only getting worse
Words and people speaking those words torment you
Like a storm over the ocean of your mind
Endless days and nights
Until one day the sea settles
And the opportunity is taken to be as free
As the fish flying past you

Natalie Anne Deller
Corpus Christi, TX

When You Were Born

When you were born
My life changed
Irrevocably and profoundly
Beyond my knowledge or comprehension

I watched as you were pushed and pulled into this plane
I stood witness to the moment you came to be
I knew
That this had changed me

Washing over, consuming me, was a tsunami of euphoria
Higher than any drug has ever taken me
More satisfying and gratifying than any joy I'd ever felt

The energy brought into this world was coughed and cried out
Exploding in all directions a billion flechettes
fragments that cut through every inch of my body and soul
In its place was left warmth and love
A bond that solidified my spirit
That returned hope and faith into my life

And all I could do was choke back tears
And say hello

Drouin Healey
Roseville, CA

Once Upon a Tongue

We met as youngsters
and fell in love.
Passions fierce and
innocent as a dove.
We lived and laughed
while finding our way.
Decided to wed one pretty
spring day.
We wrote our vows of love
from the heart.
Promising forever to never
part.
Days, months and years
flew by.
We bore a son and happy
tears we did cry.
Time took its toll on
your once sharp mind.
Words became very hard for
to you to find.
In your last few months
you couldn't say what I
longed to hear.
Once upon a tongue,
I love you dear.

Matthew W. Sims
Shreveport, LA

Lessons from My Father

Thanks for showing me vows mean nothing
That"I love you's" always end
Thank you for teaching me to trade in my old toys
For ones that are shiny and new
You showed me that what the world says about love
Is true
"It fades""it changes" "love is not a choice"
So what if you break someone's heart
Do what is best for you
Their feelings don't matter
It's all about you
Thank you for teaching me that commitments don't matter
That if something better comes along
You can just have it
So what if you promised
So what if you said I do
Obviously those things mean nothing to you
So thank you for teaching your daughter
That love leads to heartbreak
That promises are meant to be broken
That those happy endings you read to her as a child
Never really existed

Kathryn Noelle Reeves
Antioch, TN

Strong

My need for you grew
Blossomed like flowers in the spring
And the first time you undid me
Destroyed my sense and dropped me into the abyss
I thought you were god
My bones ached for you there was a pull inside me
Pulled me to the darkness that you are
Everything hurt
but at the same time I felt nothing
because my senses were marred by your expertise
But my need for you wilted
Like flowers in the summer heat
Because I became strong

Meghan Elizabeth Ballinger
Buda, TX

Quantum Morning

Is.
Is awake. Is morning. Yawn. Stand. Look. Stretch. Sigh.
Wash. Dress. Breathe. Walk. Listen. Clear air. Bright. New.
Is outside.
Is breeze. Hear whoosh. Smooth. Cool on face. Smile.
Is path. Feel/hear breeze through shaking leaves in woods.
Is walking. Path winds. Leaves move. Sun flickers. Shadows. Walk.
Is clearing. Low grass. Small stones. Buzzing. Sun bright.
Air warm. Colors. Sit. Breathe. Rest.
Is path. Hear shhhh. Feel breeze. Sun sparkles. Squint. See rainbow.
Listen. Feel. Look. Smile. Walk.
Is birds. Hear chirps. Chirp. Tweet. Colors. Flicker. Chirp. Chuckle.
Is path. Walk home. Breeze. Sun. Warm. Bright. Breathe. Walk.
Is home. Sit. Stretch. Breathe. Rest. Smile.
Is.

Charles Dittell
Sarasota, FL

Dancing

While dancing on the moon at night
at least in thought my love I see
We glide across the treeless height
while dancing on the moon at night
Bathed forever in silver light
as hand in hand you waltz with me
While dancing on the moon at night
at least in though my love I see

Allen Watkins
The Villages, FL

The Whole Story

To reach a sound conclusion;
  Consider, first, the facts.
Not questionable information,
  Renditions of some act.
Try to visualize the whole
  Not individual sides.
Seek not just what is obvious
  Find what they'll try to hide.
Because we all are human
  We have a tendency to err.
Think back you might remember
  A time when you were there.

Suez Stubbs
Valley Springs, CA

When Is Enough Enough?

Teetering on the edge of the cliff
Tipping the scale in my favor
Looking down, my stomach twists
All food has lost its flavor
My broken spirit drowns in the abyss
This number is my identity
My self-esteem, a sliding scale
This number is the enemy.

That growling pain will go away—just need to sleep it off
Choking down the Benadryl
As I gag and start to cough
I think I might be ill...

"Sticks and stones"—they hold no weight
And yet my heart still breaks
But body shapes aren't all figure eights—
We're all different widths and lengths!

I block out their words, my head in the sand
As it sifts through the hourglass
The time has come to return to the daily impasse.
A haze of tears and confusion lifts
As I step back on the scale
I hold my breath.
When is enough enough?

Jillian Lynn Schmidt
Clinton Township, MI

Rear View Mirror

I wish the view ahead was the view in my rear view mirror
Time has been good to me
The future not so
I loved and was loved
But I reaped what I sowed
My life is empty now
The road is lined with fear
I have fond memories to hold dear

Karen Nolan
Taylor, PA

Warriors

Wounded in the battle we fight every day,
Angry we are invisible to the world where we stay.
Relationships get harder has we are trying to grow stronger,
Repair our life, repair our love,
      repair ourselves is what we are trying to do today.
Ignoring the demons in your head and fighting the fear in your heart,
Opens your eyes to a new world
      and changes the outlook to a brighter life.
Ready to be strong in the battle, fight the war to the end,
Show the world your a warrior, fearless is the target,
      indestructible is the goal.

Erin Elizabeth Haugen
Watertown, MN

The Night's Silence

I sat in the stillness
Waiting for the last of the crickets to leave
When the night was quiet
When even the ghosts were asleep
I let my body become a harmony
And my wrists a violin
And just like that I struck my bow
Again
And again
And again
And until I didn't have the courage to go on
Once again, I sat in the stillness
Waiting for the last of the audience to disappear
When the night was silent
When I went asleep

Ria Anandjee
Flushing, NY

She's Still Mom

Mom was born in the winter of 1924,
with blond hair blue eyes and a smile galore.
She was the second out of six welcomed into her home.
As a tomboy on the farmstead she would roam.
She loved sports and excelled in basketball,
but an emergency surgery put an end to it all.
So she delved into books and wrote poetry and prose.
It was the beginning of a career which gradually rose.
A stint in college she mastered her skills;
her home her priority as she dreamed of windmills.
To school the last of her ten joined the rest.
Mom wrote columns for the news; she knew she was blessed.
During decades of writing many awards she did win.
She put her heart into books her talent the pen.
Many years later she noticed the words starting to fade,
and her family worried about her memory and prayed.
Then came the time when she could not function alone,
and today she is the laughter in the nursing home.
She does not know her children but always gives them a smile.
During her 92 years of life she journeyed every mile.
Her reading has ceased and she can't recite a phrase,
but we remember what she had accomplished and we are amazed.
She once conforted her children as their problems would vary.
Mom is now content as she rocks her baby doll Mary.

Joan Benson
Monroe City, MO

Time to Fly

Who said we had no wings
The songs we sing are nothing without the melody,
Is it me? Is it love at first flight, I continue to fight but
I have nothing but faith that this time it will happen
Elevation begins with our minds
Now it is time to climb up the highest tree
Now I can see my obstacles from a birds view
Even you now appear to be small
But am I now tall? towering over my yesterdays? brave?
Now I must jump in faith that it will happen
with God as my captain
I will take the passengers seat on this flight
I repeat, I can do all things through him that strengthens me
1,2,3
he
lifted me
gliding, defying gravity, water walking strength
he propelled my wings
my dreams, I am now among
touching every one
as the vapors of clouds
living out loud
on purpose
never turning back
my first flight
will not be my last

Kimberly Gale Abdul-Malik
Sherman Oaks, CA

Voice Postponed

What happens to a voice postponed?
Does it close up,
Like the sound of a mother who lost her pup?
Does it lower in tone,
Like the sound of a father who never made it back home?
Or is it loud—
Like the scream of a child being gunned down?
Is it silent like the homeless man who was buried at the mound.
Is it written like a dream deferred,
Where a woman's voice is seen as absurd.
Does it screech like a bird,
Or is it slurred and stirred like a spoon in a prison's kitchen?
Maybe it's the baby's cries of tensions that have risen.
Does it have an unbearable stench,
Where one didn't have a seat at the bench.
Is it stitched in, like a needle and pin?
Or is it the grin that stains the skin.
Is it the chains of a world that's as empty as a bin.
Lost in the wind,
With nothing but the spin of a sin that has yet to be freed.
Nah...
What happens to a voice postponed?
It's the cries of a world disowned...

Ashleigh Janelle Holloway
Atlanta, GA

Suicide Delinquent

Captured horrified
Wrapped in flesh for clothes
Hoping just to close my eyes
Evading Satan's pose
Rising up from Hells fires
Or so that is what I'm told
Bound and gagged with my desire
To the devil my soul is sold
To save my flower
My precious bleeding rose

The rose that bleeds for me
Will be the rose that sets me free
As Satan rises from black ash
Earth's mortal beings and hell will clash
The rose that blooms will only grow
As long as blood in my veins still flow
Waging war for human sins
The end of the world from where it begins

The rose grows from between the cement
Causing me to kneel in lament
The rose that bleeds from white to red
Leaves me in suffer and torment
Because now I know
My bleeding rose
Has found peace through death

Christian Ralph Kerby
Sewell, NJ

Alone

No one to help
No one to confide
Just me and my thoughts
to decide

But my mind is not enough
so it seems
No I cannot trust
the desire beneath

Two paths which will I take
Eyes And hands roaming for help
but yet they mistake

No one is there to take my hand
And the most powerful of all
I do not deserve to before thee stand

Like a tide my energy pushes in
Moving out further, stretching from
where it began

Life leaves my eyes like droplets trailing down glass
leaving a disfigured, disruptive path

I'm alone on this road
Unsteady on my feet
I myself have to find balance
In this solitude I did not wish to seek

Veronica Denise Hamlet
Center Line, MI

Shattered

The vase shatters
as the bullet ripples
through its shell.
The flowers fall
dead upon the table
amongst the glass.
The water slowly drips
like cooling blood
onto the floor.
The glass lays
in innumerable pieces
amidst the corpses.
The room is
an absolute mess,
the scene of a murder

Annette Shukaitis
Mount Pocono, PA

Hands

5 fingers and 2 hands
Working through stone
Carving wooden homes
Molding clay tombs
Why should we wonder?
Who can we ponder?
No question for advice
2 answers would be nice
But none is better off
It leaves no leading trace
DNA is out of place
So crowded to complete
Why man is to discreet
This is why im meek
Condemned to living grace

Diana S. Karplyuk
Kent, WA

Murmur

Whispers of wasted potential
echo in your head,
while reality show demons
wreak havoc in your bed.

Amanda Seagraves
Loris, SC

The Call Bell Rings

No matter the time, no matter the day.
The call bell rings, I'm on my way!
Ready to serve and ready to please.
God, help me! I pray on my knees.
Help me think quick and ease the pain.
A level and clear head I must maintain.
To save my patient, I must stay.
Until that night they pass away.
Sorrow and heartache, I hope to ease.
Although in this game there are NO guarantees.
The pain I feel, I must contain.
Except to myself, I won't complain.
The call bell rings, I'm on my way!

Amanda Watson
The Dalles, OR

Chalk It Up to Apathy

As a kid
I'm expected
To be something
And now that I'm older
I realize I'll never be anything at all
I'm strung out and fed up with the strain
I get more anxious as each day passes
It feels like I can't win
I'm growing up and giving in
And you know what?
It hurts
"You just need to try,"
You know I do
You're under my skin
And I'm letting you fester
But it still feels like I can't win
I'm getting worse
And I might die of boredom if you don't kill me first
I realize I had every chance
I've been given every opportunity
I never thought I'd be nothing at all
And it hurts

Violet Van Buren
Upton, MA

Lincoln's Pillow

You set us free
From the black genocide.
Escorting mortality south
On the iron train of thought.
But Lincoln's pillow still bleeds.
Because we traded lives
For pennies,
And then tossed them away.

Andrew Piasecki
Hobe Sound, FL

Materialism

Sometimes in life
You must buy a toy
To get out of life
A little joy
Yet a few seldom days
You are sure you scored
When you've found a toy
Which you'll never be bored
Then you start to fret
Creating a clever ploy
To keep that thing
That you'll always enjoy

Jared Christopher Conklin
Des Moines, WA

Black Hole

Little black hole
Where does it end?
It makes me wonder
What people use it for.
Secrets big and small
Hide in the dark depths
Never to be found ever again.

Carlee Yulianna Chattin
Dahlonega, GA

Grandma

You were so amazing, kind and loving.
I remember the countless hours
You spent teaching me,
The Sunday cinnamon rolls,
Along with the board games,
And the many long talks.
You have given me so many
Fond memories that I will,
Always cherish and I thank
You for that.
You were such an amazing strong Grandma.
I love and miss you so much.
Until we meet again.

Lori Sessions-McCurdy
Monroe, UT

Finish Line

I have been walking a life
Without a life
But that we dare to imagine
That we are souls
Just walking in bodies
I know this to be true
I've lost my soul before silly to live without reason
To stammer around with sight
To have ears and a heart, but deaf to have your feelings
No passion or joy the uncomfort of only time and space
Lonely life, is just a waste
We wander in circles, get me to a higher place
The path must be flat and straight
Avoid the hurtles, bumps, and delays.
The faster the better, when we will this be over?
 I know happiness is just around the corner.
Finally we made, I can see it straight ahead it's the end.
At the finish line, look I see my family and friends.
Is this right? I don't see diamonds and gold rings.
Just warm bodies to hold.
Isn't this where I started when I first began?
I've literally ran my entire life.
It's like I was running in place.
Humans most essential foot race.

Tirena Wiles
Hamilton, NJ

Beats

Her fingers glide across the keys at speeds
Stopping hearts and holding breaths with swish of light
Creating worlds of bright and lush young leads
Fantasies and majesties from keys too bright
Drawing bows and tapping feet to beats
Conducting flows from left to right and back
And mallets striking from the back row seats
Hearing heels and clicks and clacks
Knowing feats and smiling strings and accompanies
Musicians wiping sweat in beat with hands
Calloused by their zeals for destinies
Painting pictures of timeless purple lands
Singing songs of passion and defeats
And wondering if souls could ever greet.

Shanaya Young
Lynchburg, VA

The Bigot's Heart

Dedicated to Heather Heyer
Here I stand proud and strong
Convinced I am right and you are wrong.
Confronting you with wild eyed stare
Yelling and taunting with racist flare.
With the contempt, I show for any other
I assault my sister and kill my brother.
I march before you, to do you harm
When I could have stood with you arm in arm.
The strife is over and the smoke is clear
Our blood both red and our end both near.
I stand victorious over your broken frame
Unapologetic about of my shame.
And for all my violence, I could never see
The one I hated was always me.

Ken Halley
Wichita, KS

The Falsely Imprisoned

A rock hard cave in a pitted doom,
A candle was placed in the corner and lit up the room.
From side to side a beige colored rock,
You can bang with your fists and he won't hear you knock.
Air seeps in through the creases of the door,
A blanket is placed against cold feet to the floor.
Under the ground, not too far from the sky,
You may hear her slither, but you won't hear him cry.
And so they wait and wonder why,
So many could care less, while so many lie.
They put their faith in paper trails,
And wait for senders whose letter still mails.
Excited for some candy treat,
Or some form of protein left in the meat.
Clean water may be hard to find,
But they will live till tomorrow if the false imprisoner is kind.
They wait on a man, instead of the Lord,
To rescue them free from the gun or the sword.
And as the years continue to pass,
They forgot that they didn't need to pray at a Sunday school mass.

Kristie Anne Raccuglia
Marco Island, FL

I Miss You

I miss you
Not just your body or the warmth of your lips on mine
I miss your presence
That feeling of safety and comfort I get when I'm with you
I miss being able to look up and smile
Because there is nowhere I would rather be than in your arms
I miss laughing
Because the happiness inside me is bubbling over
I miss looking into your eyes
Those deep, beautiful eyes
And knowing that our love cannot be broken simply by distance
We are stronger than that
We have the unbreakable bond that is our longing to be together
Yet still
I miss you

Olivia Rose Cheslock
Jonestown, PA

A Heartbeat That Never Beats!

A beauty that is forever lost in the mist of the afterlife
A soul that we may no longer see
A home that can never truly be filled
Tears that always hide so deep inside
they start to melt you down until all that's left is
agony, misery, sorrow and defeat
A deep anger takes over and tries to confuse and consume you
It's like a circle that stops it circulation midair
Afraid to move, afraid to breathe afraid to live
Do you jump? Do you wait?
No time to think adrenaline is in motion
All your feelings, all your thoughts, all your words disappear
Still in the air falling further and further
in the hole that you created
That one word that could've saved you but no one there to hear it
That one chance you had to say it, but pride got in the way
Now you have to live another day knowing your chance faded away . . .

Marie Dobbins
Jamestown, NY

You Are Not Alone

You hide behind a "thank you shield" and mask of confidence
so that the world will never see
the torment your soul is racked with.
They see your smile, so timid and gentle voice, so kind.
They don't realize deep inside you, there are voices in your mind.
You hold a gleaming silver sword and gauntlets on your arms
To hide the words of hatred pure and fresh, new battle scars.
You're longing for a sweet escape from the cruelties of our world
And build up walls to hide yourself from pains and hurt untold.
Now here I am right at the base and long to enter in
to hold you close and whisper sweet that you are not alone.
You're important. You are worth it.
You are loved more than you know.
I'm right here, right beside you. I won't leave you alone.
You mean the world to me and I would miss you if you left.
Please, let yourself feel peace my love.
Don't give in to the trap.
Yes, you've stumbled. I know you have.
That doesn't mean you're weak or less than worthy of the blessings
for which your aching soul doth seek.
Hold on a little longer; give up the ball and chain.
Lift up your eyes and free yourself from all your inside pain.
Now dry your tears, close your eyes, read these words and know
I'm always right beside you, love.
You are not alone.

Aurelia Ellsworth
Mesa, AZ

The Narrow Path

I died to be a dreamer
I died to get away
I never asked for this
I only needed a say
I only wanted a life
I only needed a day
Just a little time
Just one more way
If you could see me now
I bet you'd surly cry
You may have survived
But in the end you'll always die
You may be living now
But what's the point in that
Standing on a dead earth
You just look flat
The longer you stay here
The shorter the ride in the hearse
Because you were born this way
There will be no gold, frankincense, myrrh
You deserve nothing
You deserve the shame
You deserve the agony when you die in vain
And He will rule with justice
And cast those to His right and left
And those to His right will follow Him
And those to the left follow death

Katherine Jurbala
Oviedo, FL

More Like a Window

When is a mirror just a mirror?
Well it never quite is, you see.
It is surely underestimated,
The power it conceals beneath
It is much more like a window,
But with an ever changing scene.
A window that may gaze deep;
Into your soul, if you please.
But one will never see an image
The same as another human being.
Odd to ponder on that thought,
Wondering, how could that possibly be?
This is the thought that most overlook;
Why some are trapped without a key,
Because emotions control the image
That every individual chooses to see.
Emotions see before the eyes,
And the eyes just choose to agree.
So a mirror is never just a mirror,
And that it will never ever be.

Kayla Roberts
Saugus, CA

Why?

There's so much that's changed in my life.
So much, I'm not sure anymore what is right.
My home has been falling apart;
it seems so many of us have lost our heart.
What happened to all that we fought for?
To freedoms, hopes, and dreams.
How could we forget we're a potluck of hopeful beings?
Why are we doing these things?
We used to be safe on our streets, in our skins;
on our own two feet.
Now fear rules everything.
It seems our tactics have retreated.
We're back to fighting with hatred.
Why are we doing these things?
We once loved and showed what was right;
and now all we do is fight.
Complaining about money, and power.
No one seems to care about our limited hours.
We're dying slowly, day by day.
Our earth is slipping away.
And all we do is kick and scream at each other.
Why are we doing these things?

Melissa Lynn Phipps
Abingdon, VA

Sunshine

I have never seen a flower like you.
Having the whole world silent at your roots.
The dirt released an essence that sang into the sky.
The wind danced to a tune that only you could create.
Pricking sinister hands,
you were beautiful.
Winter came and I stayed inside.
An ache in my heart and an ache in my mind.
It was a constant worry that you would not survive.
Tell me, what did you dream of?
I saw stars,
but none as bright as your petals.
I felt clouds,
but none as delicate as your caress.
I basked in the moonlight,
and I could hear your laughter.
Thank you for being alive.
Without you, I would not know how to live.
And so I part,
but I will never let the world
take away my Sunshine.

Annie Feng
Metairie, LA

I Hate

I hate the way you hurt me
I hate the way you lie
I hate the way you push me away
I hate the way you make me cry.
I hate when you destroy my trust
I hate when you disappear
I hate when you won't answer me
I hate when you leave me in fear.
I hate how your always on my mind
I hate how you break my heart
I hate how you mess me up
I hate how you can rip me apart.
I hate that I need you so much
I hate that I forgive everything you do
I hate that I can't stay mad
I hate that I don't want to be without you.
I hate that my love is blind
I hate that you know it too
I hate that no matter what you do to me
I hate that I don't hate you.

Amy Deason
Gentry, AR

My Friend

Is she my friend?
Or is she my worst enemy?
Sometimes I feel like I'm being pushed away into a dark alley
and I can't escape.
Should I run?
It's not her fault.
Or is it?
No but she's my best friend . . .
Or was she?

Eunice Zelaya
Mount Vernon, NY

Youth

formality has become a reality.
sexuality has brought my attention to modality.
hospitality showing liberality.
demanding, defending your rights.
musicality can bring spirituality to good use.
caring, bearing my hopes to the young ones.
collecting, projecting what's my next path toward the youth.

Jessa Agustin
Kent, WA

Breath of Grace

I'm on a eagle's flight
Not searching for a fight
Soul diving within hell& grace
Must escape from this despaired stage
Some kind of solace to mend me
Emptiness won't bend thee
Cold sore heart alongside a divine shining sun
Flying fearless on an eagle's back weighing a ton
Composing a song of peace to seal my fate
As I savor your breath of grace.

Craig J. Burt
Milwaukee, WI

The Crow

This weed is the key
Oh how it numbs me
Never taking the constant pain away
Only dulling it so that it might remain
Because the pain is how I maintain
With this strain so strong
I right my wrongs, sing these words like a song
For if I'm right ...I'm wrong

Mary Nicole Montgomery
Fresno, CA

Sunrise

Lonely stars drowning in inky-black sea
A fragile crescent of moon is battered
This once-familiar shape is now lost to me
Once carefully placed points are scattered
Orion, brave and strong, now lost and confused
The sky's peaceful canvas in turmoil
The Painter withdraws, his artwork abused
Corrupted beauty is abandoned to spoil
A twilight breeze ushers in notes of grief
Mourning loss and fear in changing times
The cry of the ocean calls for relief
Trees whisper for peace in primitive rhymes
A soft glow shatters the tenebrous night
Tendrils of sun grasp for pieces of day
Gently assembling an arrangement of light
Building up hope in exquisite array

Rachel Elizabeth Morand
Zionsville, IN

Gymnastics

Flip, split, balance, swing,
Glide just like an eagle's wing,
Flip so high the world goes by,
Faster than a cheetah's eye.

Korynn Laughlin
Phillipston, MA

Frost Bites

It's so cold in here.
It's getting colder still,
reading the writing on the other side
of these foggy eyes.
So foggy no one sees inside,
but just the writings of those who have tried.
Yet when your eyes meet mine
you can look through the letters.
There you will find
a freezing child,
asking if its alright
to come outside
while hes still alive.

Mason Fordyce
Trotwood, OH

Here's to the Girls

Here's to the girls that aren't pink and frilly, but black and plaid.
The ones who are fall and winter instead of spring or summer.
Here's to the girls who are clumsy and awkward.
Who don't have the right amount of freckles dusting their nose,
but bags under their eyes.
Their eyes hold swamps and coals instead of the oceans and gold.
Those who don't go to parties whether by choice or not.
Here's to the girls who are sunflowers instead of roses,
the ones choosing to be a coming storm rather than a raging fire.

Samantha Cheyenne Lecocq
San Marcos, CA

Under the Stars

When we lay under the stars
I will use your skin as my map.
I will trace every inch of your flesh.
I will reveal all the places where we will go.
In the meantime you can tell me
where we have been, so I don't
retrace the same steps.
We will go somewhere new, a place
with a different view.

Katarina Berisaj
Novi Mi, MI

Woman Thou Are Loose

Loose from chains and shackles that try to bind you.
Loose from every fear and torment
That try to take hold of your inner being.
Loose from every abuse that diminishes your self- esteem.
Oh woman of God come forth, come forth.
Like wings of an eagle soar to the height of your destiny.
Be still and know that I am God.
I will exalt you in due time.
Woman of God my hand is upon you.
I call you in your mother's womb.
Break free, break free, stand tall.
Release your inhibitions and desires.
Walk into your authority and take hold of your dreams.
Until they manifest.
Dream, dream woman of God.

Sanjanetta Harris
Jacksonville, FL

Guilty

We teach girls shame
That showing skin is a distraction
That their bodies are made to be hidden
That they are to blame for any inappropriate advances
If her shorts were longer
If her shoulders were covered
If she wasn't out late
If she acted a bit more confident
He feeds the investigators excuse after excuse
"I just couldn't control myself!" Of course he couldn't
How could I hold him responsible when it was my fault?
Honestly, I should have enjoyed it
I just had to go and make a big deal out of nothing
But it wasn't just nothing
We are taught how to avoid rape
When we should be taught to not rape at all
No one asks for this violation
No one asks for this type of pain
I can't help but think as I try to hide
That promoting changes to prevent rape
Is the same thing as saying
"Rape the other girl"
Stop victim blaming
Stop making pretence into an artform
Stop making me afraid to say 'No'
But above all, stop making me feel guilty

Thayer Cumings
Bristow, VA

Who Am I?

Uncertain
   about the fabric of me.
   my skin is unblemished,
   genetically passed down
   to me by some mother
Who
   gave birth to me. Some
   mother who gave me up,
   hoping she was doing the
   right thing. My hair
is
   enviable - blonde strands
   naturally highlighted with
   gold. What I'm more than a
   little vague about is
the stranger
   who keeps insisting
   she is the real me,
   and if I would allow
   her to take up residence
inside
   this cowardly shell,
   I will finally come
   to terms with who
   I was born to be.

Faith Elizabeth Hansen
Gilbert, AZ

Elude

I am the summons of chaos,
Beast amongst hordes.
I'm a jack of all trades yet a master of none.
I am diseased.

Purged words feed the red,
seeing faces of living dead.
Young and old and all around,
dancing merrily about town.
With a glass they raise
to the tides, they give cheer,
all not knowing what evils lie near...

but the end is at hand to one all fare and near....

Ron Lee Farra
La Mirada, CA

You Are My Moon

I want to be your sun,
for you are my moon.
Our love is like a rose bush,
bold and beautiful, but our thorns
don't let anyone break through.
They say "Two is better than one"
but I know that isn't true.
For now that we are married,
I will forever be one with you.
I love to make you happy,
especially when it gets hard,
for your smile on the toughest days,
makes me feel as though I built
the highest tower of playing cards.
I know you may not realize this,
but what I'm saying is true:
at night I get so scared I could
never sleep without you.

Brooke Autum Johnson
Milwaukee, WI

Feelings, the Figure De Proue

I.
They are too much supper
And never enough. The stomach
Drops as does a basket of apples too heavy for the
Hands that carry it. Yet, each green orb is
So delightful, that to pluck even one from
Its woven nest seems wasteful.
I do not intend to feed the birds.
II.
Intensity of Romantic Hope never comes
To dinner without her companion, Fear of Rejection.
Their arms link in reluctant solidarity, and
Are perhaps the archetype for co-dependency.
Together they feed Anxiety, which is
Cyanide for hope. But Trust is
In the orchard climbing
Apple trees and filling baskets,
Her pockets, and
Calls down to her companions to
Bring the wheelbarrow too.

Jamie King
Colorado Springs, CO

Fractures

You have taken with you my Sun
The stars, packed in bags of duffelled canvas
Those low hanging clouds caught in the nettings of your eye
You have dragged the blue to furthest reaches
To places I can not follow, covered
With scraps of dead leaves and gangrenous petals
The ends of odds are odds and ends
In cessation of hard covered songs and dances
Delicate filigree wrap around my warring fingers
Lacework of entanglements latticed dreams
Gateways to the heavens now strain unyielding
The way of parted fractures lay raw and bleeding in soot
Paint my eyes in the opaques of this darkening water
Barring the seams of full lips, a spiritless cadaver
Amidst the dimming of the burnished essence of living coals
When upon the wake of that new dawn, You were turned to dust

Felicia M. Elmanfaa
Philadelphia, PA

A Rootless Tree

Trees are rarely still, they dance in the wind
Free as the wind itself, though fixed by their roots
A haven for all, a home for some
They dance, they drink, and they die by their roots

I sit here watching hearing the Harbour
Feeling the cracked, dry roots and so I wonder
I wonder of home, the place of our roots
Grounded and protected, simple and humbling

Home. What does it mean when you've travelled far
Scattered memories in an ever-tumbling jigsaw
Home has changed for me many times over
I'm still unsure of that place that's truly mine

Not the icy breath from the mountains near
Nor the crackling leaves under my footstep
Not the high city peaks amongst concrete lanes
Nor the touch of nature with stories entwined

My transplanted roots answer my questions
Of what place makes a home, and I realize
For what makes a home to me I now know
That it's not made of where, it is not made of when
but who

Erin Tunbridge
Boulder, CO

Heaven's Window

If I could peek into Heaven's window
I know this is what I would see:
Your perfect radiant smile
smiling back at me!
Telling me you're happy
and you hate to see us cry
but the void you left us with feels
like it stopped the hands of time.
You were the best of the best
and no one could ever take your place!
Yet when I'm missing you dearly
my mind drifts away to a place I'd rather be
and that's peeking through
Heaven's window
to see you smiling back at me!

Allyson Elaine Humphrey
Youngstown, OH

DNA Evolution

evolution is the marriage
of elements
and a concomito dissipation
of motion
during which surviving motion
and element
effect a parallel
transformation of material
time, change and element
together in infinite marriage
become kind deceivers
where weighty scale or bone
became downy feather
having drawn a heavy curtain
where no witness
sees the interchange,
only a fragmented echoe
buried
deep in matrix

Ned Pendergast
San Francisco, CA

Walk Away, Darkness

Walk away, Darkness
The deep pit of lies holds the mysteries of tomorrow;
The unhappiness of the world brings sorrow.
You say the war is against another,
But I say it's against each other.
We claw, we tear, we shatter,
We act like nothing is the matter.
When truly there are people hurting on the inside;
They're dying from a world filled with formaldehyde.
People take others happiness, because they can't find their own.
People starve themselves until they're dry bone.
We've crumbled up and shriveled away from our mess.
Is it because we've fallen into darkness?

Darkness, whatever do you mean?
Whenever I see darkness, I see a teen.
She walks through the hall with her head hung low;
Ask if she's okay and she'll say no.
But you just give her a pat on the back and go.
Darkness, why do you mention?
Whenever I see darkness, I feel tension.
Walking past you I feel the hate in the air;
You talk bad about me because you seem to still care.
Can I walk away from the darkness, or will it walk from me?
If only I could lock it away, and throw out the key.
Darkness.

Kynnedy Marie Roller
O'Fallon, IL

Trifecta

My feet pound the earth,
A locomotive of flesh and bone,
Thus far has carried me,
Since my troublesome birth.
Crying is my heart; palpitating and urging me to
Grant it an audience . . .

The silence screams through brush,
A menagerie of unknowns,
Has stalked me along the way,
I panic, sensing their touch.
Quivering is my mind; collapsing and begging me to
Acknowledge the dangers . . .

Diamonds glow with hunger,
Ambers know me and my scent,
Strength and instinct along the path,
Keeps them from tearing me asunder.
Panting are the wolves; salivating and wishing me to
Surrender to my fatigue . . .

The thicket reveals an escape,
A beacon on a twisted coast,
Angels turn away in fright,
Oh God, is now too late?
Wavering is the future; bending and imploring me to
Survive . . . just survive . . .

Mark Andrew Manning
Saraland, AL

Chasing Footsteps

Black pavement beneath my feet
I've been walking the same road for a while
something has changed

your steps fall ahead of me
now behind
no longer in tune with mine

this road, once fresh and thriving
is now worn
the cracks get covered, only to be torn anew

this black pavement is running out of time
why was it always so hard for you to match
your footsteps with mine?

Lydia E. Hoesing
O'Neill, NE

I Am a Tomato

Some think I am a fruit
Some a vegetable
Personally, I can go either way
Trying to figure out who I am day by day
I am a tomato
I am the color of passion
Love
Fire
Powerful on the outside, soft on the inside
Making it hard to know what I keep confined
I am a tomato
I'm not the tallest
I'm not the smartest
Not the best
But my fiery skin will make sure I beat out all the rest

I am a tomato

Jenna Christine Pupillo
Schwenksville, PA

It's Her Fault, You Say

"It's her fault," you say,
because if she didn't smile,
in such a nice way
he would have walked away.
Because if she didn't wear
such a pretty display,
he would not have seen her as prey.
Because if her clothes didn't convey
that she seeks
attention in every single way
he would have looked away.

Because boys will be boys
and men,
men will always be the same.
Their reputations
we cannot defame,
and their masculinity,
too fragile for this filthy game.

But women,
women are always to blame
for the temptations
that men cannot tame.

Salma Elztahry
Kendall Park, NJ

Love Through Time

His eyes allured at what he saw,
In a tattered city, he was in awe.
A graceful charming woman lit the path,
The angle pure, he sought to hath.
In a blue gown and a scarf clear white,
O' her beauty cleansed the entire sight.
Almighty himself thought not feasible,
A commoner and a noble just unforeseeable.
In spite of this, their bond strong,
Their love eternal as a song.
Their oath a canvas that few dismiss,
One most beautiful by a paramour's bliss.
Lords and Nobles will enrage,
Thus the couple will set to flames.
Ash will fade and fire will dwindle,
But couple's love will always kindle.

Liel Avraham
University Heights, OH

Birds, Cats, Dogs, and Fleas

I'm sometimes amused by words and how
  they're used.
Like in the spring, when birds are on the
  wing.
But isn't that absurd, I thought the wings
  were on the bird.

Then I look up and see a crow in a tree,
  flapping his wings and cawing at me.
I'll bet you money that he thinks is funny,
  but he'll get his, wait and see.

They say a turkey you can dress.
  With a Tutu I guess.
No, you dummy, it's stuffing for his tummy.

Oh look! Did you see that dog on the "flea",
  Chased by a cat meaner than he?

Oh well, I like to rhyme. It kills the
  time, while I laugh at that dog on
  the"flea".

Roy Darrel James
Longview, WA

Untitled

As you look out at this beautiful view
Reflecting on all the things that have passed
There is simply nothing you can do
To make what you have desired most to last

So look within yourself, in your own heart
It may seem like this is the journey's end
How can you tell this is not just the start
One can't know what is just around the bend

Now take a look at all that you have done
Everything that you hold near and dear
Can you not see that it is like the sun
That you may not have a single fear

Now look up and the clear and blue blue sky
Let it release, all the pain can now fly

Chrysania Miller
Grace, ID

Success

I've got to
I've got to try
I need to
For me.

My memories
Are of happy days
Filled with self-reliance
So, tomorrows
Can be filled
With happiness
Which undeniably accompanies
SUCCESS
When earned with
Honesty
Perseverance
Faith
And drive
Yet, finally
So naturally
With love—

Which comes from
Peace of mind.

Petra Thorne
Greenville, SC

2017

On a cold and blistery January morn; I watch the flames lick the logs as I gaze through the fire before me. Another year has begun.

Just like the one before it, I am sure this one will travel with equal speed to it's destined end. As it goes it will gather the memories of pain and sorrows, the joys of the morrows, of good times, and tearful ones, of loved ones, and sad goodbyes.

Life has a way to bring these properties into focus, whether we are ready for them to be or not. We can wallow in depression or face them head on, and be strong in our faith. I choose to let God lead me where I need to be!

Oh look! Though the wind is blowing and drying up the earth, the sun is out!

Jennie Knies
Erie, CO

Arise and Shine

And darkness covered my spirit and soul
Until he spoke and said
Let there be light
To the depression that held me
So I crawled out of the dark hole
That I dug for myself
As a little child to escape
The painful life I chose to take
Until 40 years later
The God of the Universe
Helped me to become a lover
And no longer a hater
Now I lay open my heart and soul
So others may see the life
That is there for the taking
Not living in dread but rather
A spiritual awakening
Come now ask of me
How this came about
Like Lazarus from the tomb
When the Lord did shout.

Michael Herbst
Ogdensburg, NY

Untitled

The election is finally over
News anchors have nothing to cover
The people have spoken
We all know campaign promises are broken
As a Nation we will heal
Many are afraid of repeal
We must respect the law
Hopefully law and order can be restored
We must give the President-elect a chance
To keep jobs in America was his stance
Buy "USA" if you can A job for Americans is the plan
Keep these jobs here and not overseas
Comes from the "forgotten man" with his pleas
Let us keep America first
We are "number one" not the worst.

Julie Gronowetter
Woodmere, NY

Index of Poets

9 781608 806270